How to L... the Life you Love

and love the life you live

How to Live the Life you Love

and love the life you live

James Gladwin

Bene Factum Publishing

Published in 2000

by

Bene Factum Publishing

11a Gillingham Street

London

SW1V 1HN

Tel: + 44 (0)20 7630 8616

Fax: + 44 (0)20 7630 5202

www.benefactum.co.uk

ISBN 0-9522754-7-3

Design and Typesetting by
Tom Grzelinski & Adam Meredith of Polka. Creation

Printed Midas UK Ltd

The quotation from Shantideva is from The Way of the Bodhisattva,
translated by the Padmakara Translation Group, published by Shambala Press.
The quotation at the beginning of the Sixth morning is from
"Sophie's World" by Jostein Gaarder

A CIP catalogue record of this book is available
from the British Library.

"People say that what we're all experiencing is the meaning of life... I think what we're really experiencing is the experience of being alive."

Contents

Introduction

This book has deep roots, and owes its sustenance to many, many people. It reflects almost every period of my experience, and those people I know, and love.

There are some groups, and individuals, however, to whom I must express particular acknowledgement: the three Benedictine communities at Ampleforth, England, St. Louis and St. Meinrad in the US. My colleagues at Hoggett Bowers, Goddard Kay Rogers, the DHC Group, and The Centre for High Performance. My publisher Anthony Weldon, my editor, Katy Brown and the book's designer, Tom Grzelinski.

My own, especial, family.

And T, without whose support, encouragement and enduring love not one word could have been written.

Above all, I am mindful of Shantideva's wisdom:

What I have to say has all been said before,
And I am destitute of learning and of skill with words.
I therefore have no thought that this might be of benefit to others;
I wrote it only to sustain my understanding.

For errors of grammar and style, I apologise; for shortcomings of insight, I am responsible.

JFG
Bath, Somerset

First evening

Setting Out - What You Need to Pack

> Today is the beginning of an exciting journey. You may feel a variety of emotions: hope, anticipation, cynicism, weariness, excitement. Allow these and many other feelings to well up from your heart and flow where they will......
>
> We are all born to live a life that we love, and the process of becoming fully alive will be different for each one of us because we are special, unique individual men and women who are designed to become fully alive.

Welcome: this book is for you! Learning how to live the life you love is the most worthwhile project you can undertake. Of course, there are so many other important activities which compete for your time - family, relationships, money, health, romance - that loving the life you live can get submerged, even forgotten. Yet nothing else in your life will work satisfactorily for you unless you understand the ingredients that go towards making a life that is perfect for you.

How to use this book

There are different ways to use this book, and it is a book to be <u>used</u> rather than simply read. You might like to start at the beginning, and work through, each day, to the end. Or you could dip into sections that appeal immediately to you, and start from there. You could check out the index and find a topic that catches your eye. Whichever way, every section has a similar layout, covering a topic, with checklists, with some question and answer sessions, and a summary at the end.

It is important to stress, however, that we are all beginners when it comes to learning to live lives that we love. This is very valuable to remember, because it may help you to relax and enjoy the journey.

As a beginner, you can allow yourself to make mistakes, to wander a bit from the path, to pitch your tent where you want to, rather than where the map says you should.

So you are not going to be spending the next 21 days in boot camp, taking part in gruelling fitness workouts and forced marches. This book is not an engineering printout that says: "You must do it like THIS! There is NO other way!"

Rather, imagine that you are surfing the Internet and come across a website that you find interesting. Or, think of it as switching channels on the TV without knowing what you want to watch, and you come across a programme which has already begun but that suddenly catches your attention.

In one way, the life you are leading is just like that TV programme. After all, your life has already begun! And, unless

The real voyage of discovery consists not in seeking new landscapes, but in having new eyes

Marcel Proust

you have extraordinary powers of memory, you will not be able to remember the beginning! But there comes a time - perhaps it is this very moment - when life "catches your attention". This is a very powerful moment.

At such times, for a momentary instant, you are totally focused on what catches your attention. It could be the sparkle of sunlight on raindrops, or a glimpse of an attractive person stepping into a cab, or the sudden aroma or freshly baked bread. All other thoughts or distractions or worries are forgotten. Your whole attention is focused in one particular way.

You can access that same power when you bring all your focus on your life. On you.

When you take time to think about your life, it is a bit like standing on one side of a wonderful valley which stretches far ahead. You can look behind and see the journey you have taken so far. And maybe you can just see your journey's end on the horizon, shimmering in the haze of a beautiful spring day. All around you, exotic birds call to one another and flit through sun dappled trees, and you can feel the warm sun on your back.

Life Choices

While you can just make out your goal, however, it might not be so easy to know exactly the best route to take to get there. Do you go straight down the mountain path that lies at your feet, and disappears around the boulder and the corner of the trail? It is well trodden, and looks as though many other people have passed this way before. Or do you strike across the ravine, following a narrow track which seems to twist and turn following the banks of a fast flowing stream? While you are making up your mind, consider another possibility. What if you choose to follow one path, but then break off to make your own progress, and then catch another trail?

In the same way, this is how this book aims to support your journey of discovery, because this is your life. Not mine. Not your neighbour's. Not your boss's. Not your partner's. It is your life, in all its dazzling patchwork of successes, near misses, mountain vistas and dramatic canyons. It is your journey, and this book - for the next twenty-one days - is your friend and companion.

How to enjoy the next 21 days

Make the next twenty-one days enjoyable. Decide to get the sleep you need, eat sensibly, exercise suitably, and deal with issues that arise calmly and from a position of serenity.

Here is a way to help you do that.

Contract with Yourself

I, _____ commit myself to the next twenty-one days to discover how I can live the life that I love. I understand that there may be issues that confront me, and moments of doubt and uncertainty.

I undertake to look after my well being, to take my values seriously, and to give time each day to reflective reading.

I also undertake to consider the exercises and learning points as they apply to me and my life, and put them into practice authentically and intentionally.

Signed _____ Date _____

The word "contract" means "something that pulls two people or things together". In everyday life, a contract is a document that "pulls" different people to an agreement. This contract is made with yourself, and it is going to draw you towards the life you love by reminding you of your desire to do so.

The wheel of life

This is a quick and useful way to begin the next twenty-one days. And this quick exercise can be used at anytime when you feel rattled, uncertain about your feelings, or fearful about the future but are not able to say why.

Take a sheet of clear paper, and draw a circle. Divide it into eight equal segments.

Label each segment: my love and relationships; my work; my finances; my past; my quality of life; my spirit; my "now"; my well being.

Next, quickly give each segment a "score" out of ten, based on how you're feeling right now about each topic. In other words, don't think about it too much, just instinctively mark the wheel.

Love and relationships: people in my life (or not).

My work: enjoyment of career, job, current occupation or job search.

My finances: income, spending money, debt, credit cards, savings etc.

My past: unfinished business - parents, former work colleagues, unpaid taxes, something you feel ashamed about?

My quality of life: my environment, my lifestyle, how things are going for me.

My spirit: my spiritual awareness (not necessarily religion); my sense of synchronicity; my intuition; how at ease I am with discussions about wider/deeper values and insights.

My "now": how I feel right this instant.

My well being: eating sensibly. Sleeping enough. Dependency on alcohol/tobacco or other recreational drugs. Hooked on coffee. Using banned substances.

The value of this exercise is that you quickly see how your life is at this moment. And, rather than being a wheel that will roll smoothly and effortlessly, it is likely to provide a very bumpy ride because it is not a round wheel at all, but uneven segments joined together.

The point is - although you may often feel "down" or "fed-up" or "depressed" it can be hard to put our finger on exactly what it is that it going wrong.

Or you may have got into the habit of jumping too quickly to one conclusion - "I haven't got enough money" or, "I don't have a partner" or, "I'm exhausted" - without giving yourself time to look at the larger picture.

The "wheel of life" exercise allows you to quickly get a sense of your life in its entirety.

If we do not change our direction,
we are likely to end up where we
are headed

Chinese poem

When you live a life that you love, your circle is full and complete and your life works smoothly. And, more importantly, your "circle of life" is expanding to include every person and activity you can imagine!

Question: Do I have to read each section in order, and at the time of day that each section is written, like first evening, second morning and so on?

Answer: Some people prefer to dip into the book, and look at sections that immediately appeal to them. Most people find, however, that after skimming a few pages in order to get a "feel", it works best to begin at the beginning, and work through each section in order. You do not have to read at specific times of day - they are simply suggestions to give yourself time to think about the ideas, and put them into practice.

Question: I'm pretty busy right now, and weekends are really crowded what with the children and so on. Does the book have to be read absolutely every day?

Answer: Not at all! In fact, each "day" referred to in the book might well take a couple of days or a week, or even a month, for one of the ideas to take root, sprout and come to fruit in your life. Remember, much of what prevents you living lives that you love has been part of your inner furniture for many, many years. It is not going to be easy to shift the furniture around overnight! You've got used to your interior decoration and outer landscape. So it could well be that several sections "strike home" more than others, and you will give more time to those.

Question: I often buy books like this, thinking that each one will be THE answer. And, somehow, they aren't! What suggestions do you have?

A nswer: No book is for ever! It would be like your eating at one restaurant or sticking to one set of clothes for the rest of your life. Each book you have bought in the past has been of some value, and you got something from it. Hopefully it will be the same with this one, and you will find other books that reinforce some of the insights you read here, and some sections here that confirm hunches you got elsewhere. Everything that grows needs to be sown at some stage, so enjoy what you read, use what is of value, and honour what has come before.

Q uestion: I'm afraid I still feel pretty cynical about all this: I have a yammer-yammer voice inside my head saying "It's impossible to live a life I love - it just isn't realistic". Can you say a little about that?

A nswer: Healthy scepticism is a good thing; it's a good starting point to be honest about your mixed feelings towards the possibility of living the life that we love. On the other hand, it is a mistake to allow life's bruises from the past to shape our future. So, don't resist the yammer-yammer voices in your head. They think they're helping! Just see if you can turn the volume down a bit, and maybe allow some other, quieter, voices to have their say as well. Voices that suggest hope, possibility, vitality, peace, love, calm - don't drown them out.

Summary

It's OK to have a mixture of conflicting feelings about trying to live a life that you love. Don't fight them, accept that there are probably good reasons from the past for being suspicious; be gentle with yourself.

Copy the contract, sign and date it, and put it somewhere in your home or in your work area where you can often see it. And why not make it into a fun statement, using different colours or sticking positive images you can cut from magazines?

Complete your "wheel of life", and become skilful at adapting it for your own life, feeling free to change labels to personalise it for yourself.

Second evening

Limiting Expectations - What You Need to Leave Behind

> When we sense a trickle of possibility beginning to flow in our lives, we sometimes notice how we have built blocking dams across the stream of our life. But we can begin to move beyond the limits we have inadvertently set for ourselves.

How many times have you gone on holiday and found that you have taken far too many belongings? In the expectation that the resort climate (in summer) might also have snow, you packed sensible winter wear (just in case) and also those extra thick woollens (you never know) and - better be safe than sorry - you took that holdall to carry hiking boots.

It is the same with women's bags, and men's briefcases. Of course we carry a lot of useful stuff, but we seem prepared to risk posture and energy by carrying around so many extra bits and pieces that might conceivably come in useful.

Out of date beliefs

Similarly, we all carry around stuff in our heads and hearts which is often long past its "sell-by" date only to get in the way when we are learning to live lives that we love.

One reason that we go on carrying junk around with us is that it is very, very precious to us! We have been carrying it around for so long it must be important! And yet the longer we do so, the more we collect, and the heavier our burden. There comes a moment when we need to place it all gently on the ground, stretch up to the sky, and feel the lightness of heart and inner freedom that comes from not being burdened by the past.

But we haven't got there yet. Don't throw those heavy items away! Just decide not to carry them for the next 20 days. Leave them behind, ready for your return - if you still need them!

Here is a list of some limiting beliefs and expectations:

The statement below is true for me...

	sometimes	always	never
...I have to be nice to people			
...I must be kind			
...I must be perfect			
...I mustn't say "No"			
...I mustn't make a mistake			
...I ought to think of others			
...I should do more			
...I mustn't eat sweets			
...I'm not good enough			
...I'm not strong enough			
...I'm not enlightened enough			
...I'm greedy			
...I mustn't raise my voice			
...I must be the best			
...I have to earn more			
...I have to be the main breadwinner			
...I have to be right			
...I should know everything			
...I mustn't cry			
...I must have the answer			

14

Where were most of your ticks?

"Shoulds" and "Musts" and "Oughts"

Notice the words "should" and "must" and "ought" . These three words are like controls on a CD player. The volume control is extremely useful until teenagers have a sleepover and decide to experiment with the amplifier deck at two-thirty in the morning! And, when the bass, treble or mute controls are increased to their maximum, the original sound also gets distorted.

Here is an example of how "must" and "should" and "ought" distort your life.

Knowing how to discover information is a key lifetime skill. It is vital in a changing employment marketplace when the job you hold now could be downsized in five years' time. But if you become someone who must know everything, or who should know, or who ought to know, the skill has become distorted.

In practice, this means that your relationships with colleagues, children, or friends become negatively affected because you always have to be 'right' and will never be able to admit that you are "wrong", or simply don't know the answer to a particular question.

A spacious life

First, look at the list on the next page.

What has happened is that you have turned down the life-controls labelled "must", "should" and "ought". In fact, they are set to zero. In terms of your lifetime journey, you've left them behind.

...I can understand	...I am great as I am
...I can cry	...I think of others
...I am perfect	...I look fine
...I enjoy eating sweets	...I am growing in enlightenment
...I can handle whatever comes	...I express myself appropriately
...I enjoy my food	...I value my intelligence
...I value my best try	...I can see myself enjoying more
...I honour my feelings	prosperity
...I can be kind	

When you turn the must/should/ought volume down, the "music" of the list above is utterly different. There is freedom, space and room for growth.

This is what you discover as you begin to live lives that you love. Self-imposed rules and expectations that constrict your ability to be fully alive will dominate you less and less.

So you need to cultivate a "beginner's mind" for your journey, and begin unpacking the "I know where I'm heading" beliefs and expectations and leave them on one side.

The fact is, you probably can't actually imagine what it will be like to lead a life that you love because there is a tiny but insistent voice saying, "Aw, c'mon, you don't really believe that is possible, do you? You've got to be joking. I mean, it's a nice idea, but......"

Limiting beliefs and expectations are all variations on distorted musts and shoulds and oughts.

Four things come not back: the
spoken word, the sped arrow, time
past, the neglected opportunity

Omar Ibnal-Halif

Key Suggestion

Limiting beliefs are not bad, or wrong. They do not indicate something that you should feel bad about. But they do swirl around you like midges on a summer's evening. If you thrash your arms and work up a sweat - well, you know the result.

So you need to learn to be gentle on yourself, keep a sense of humour and not pass judgement one way or the other: just let them go, and put them to one side. After all, they have probably been part of your life for a long time, and will have played their part in bringing you to this moment when you choose to move on.

Remember - lay those limiting beliefs down gently.

Stretches for the Second Evening

There are moments every day when you need to stand up, walk about, clear your mind, stretch your muscles, breathe deeply and regain vitality and energy. Cats and other animals do it naturally; small children often remind us of the joy of stretching simply for the fun of it.

This "stretching exercise" works in the same way with beliefs and expectations which you may have allowed to get a bit flabby.

Although you can read the following paragraphs, the stretch is more powerful if you actually do the exercise. You will only need a notebook - word processors do not seem to work so well.

Take a few moments when you know you will not be interrupted. Put the phone on answer, and turn off the radio. Find somewhere comfortable to sit which will not make you feel sleepy.

Look at the following list of expectations and beliefs, and choose ONE that appeals to you.

I love the life that I live.

I have the skills and abilities to enjoy a wonderful life.

I am good looking

I am...

Now, copy that belief out in your notebook. As you do so, notice any thoughts or inner voice that arises as you are writing. Enjoy using the pen or pencil, take your time to "play" with the words as they appear before you.

Do the same exercise again. Write out the belief. Notice your reactions. Maybe there is not a thought, more a kind of feeling in your body. Don't react. Don't judge. Just go on writing.

Do it once again. Write out the belief. Allow yourself to feel whatever you feel. It may be a tingling of quiet excitement. It could be a feeling of anxiety. Just let them be.

And go on doing the exercise. In fact, write out the belief you have chosen 20 times. Don't rush; don't hurry. Just write normally, without trying to write beautifully or in any special way. No one is going to mark your work or assess your handwriting!

The thing always happens that you really believe in; and the belief in a thing makes it happen

Frank Lloyd Wright

When you have finished, do not rush to get up and resume your chores, or whatever you were doing previously. Allow yourself a few moments of peace just to think about the belief that you chose. Allow it to have a place in your heart, to begin to melt any hardness, and spread its healing possibility throughout your body and mind.

Learning how to stretch your belief muscles is a key component of living the life that you love. Most of us have forgotten how to do so. Over the next 20 days, you will become more and more skilful so that when you get to the end of your journey, you will understand what it means to love the live that you live.

Question: Are we always aware of our limiting beliefs? Aren't there some that are really powerful because we don't realise they are there? If so, how can we bring them into the open?

Answer: A "belief" or "the way I think about something" is rather like an iceberg. In other words, just as the tip of the berg indicates the mass of ice below the water, so a belief of which we are aware can often point to the deeper, core belief. So, gradually allowing the tip to melt allows the rest to surface and we can deal with it in our own time.

The limiting beliefs we are aware of are probably the ones to gradually let go of first - that will make room for the others.

Question: Can you say a bit more about having a "beginner's mind"? Do I really have to start at the beginning?

Answer: When we start learning something that we want to learn, we are open to every possible source of information. We don't turn down any offer of help or advice; we don't spurn any suggestions; neither do we reject a possible action out of hand. Beginners make mistakes because they don't know any better, but they don't get fussed about it either. One of the biggest obstacles to living a life that we love is that we believe we are so grown up, so mature, so sophisticated, so worldly-wise, so successful, and so damn accomplished that we have squeezed out every last drop of possibility from our lives! Until we regain our beginner's mind, we will find it pretty hard to conceive the richness and excitement of living a life that we love.

Question: You have used the word "gentle" and "gentleness" quite a few times so far. Are they kind of code words? (This question was asked by a man)

Answer: Well, not code words, but they are important. It may be a gender thing, but I notice that when men become interested in personal development and transformation issues, they tend to tackle them pretty aggressively, head-on if you like. There's a lot of effort, and struggle, and pain. On the other hand women often come across as more gentle on themselves - less "I've got to master this limiting belief thing by tonight - or else" and more, "Let's give this a chance and see what happens".

The point is this: we probably wouldn't be human if we didn't have limiting beliefs - we haven't got it all wrong just because we think such and such a thing. And letting go of these beliefs doesn't always happen overnight. An ice cube doesn't melt in an instant. And it doesn't make sense to take a hammer to the ice cube - you just get more ice. Instead, let it melt. Let those beliefs go, gently. They will, I promise

Summary

We all have limiting expectations and beliefs.

We need to begin noticing what they are, and how they impact on our lives,

We can begin cultivating a beginner's mind.

We can learn to develop a gentle approach to personal change, and a sense of humour.

Third Morning

How We Learn - Understanding Where We Give Up

Humans are very skilful at learning, but we often limit our idea of learning to school and qualifications. We have forgotten that learning comes naturally to us, and that we can continue learning in every area of our life. It might come as a shock to discover that what we learned best was - how to give up!

There is a famous parable about a cave by Plato, the Greek philosopher. In the cave is a row of people, chained in such a way that they can only face the back wall. Behind the row of people is a fire and a procession of figures walking by engaged in all the activities of life. The procession of figures casts shadows on the back wall of the cave. The people who are chained can see only the changing view of shadows, and because that is all they have ever seen, they take these shadows to be reality. Sometimes a person who is bound in this way, through great effort, manages to loosen the chains and turn around. He or she sees the fire and the procession and begins to understand that the shadows are not the reality, but merely a reflection on the wall. Perhaps with further effort that person is able to cut the chains completely and emerge into the sunlight, into freedom.

Although that story was written over 2,000 years ago, it provides a powerful description of people who "don't know any better" because they have no alternative way of understanding how everything fits together. As far as the people chained together facing the cave wall, what they are looking at and experiencing is real life. That is how life is, for them.

That parable has a lesson for us because it gives an important insight into how we think things are, and how we live our everyday lives for much of the time.

We are not actually chained facing a cave wall, but until somebody explains that the dazzling blob above our heads is the sun, we will go through life without any comprehension of the solar system. Until somebody actually sailed around our planet, everybody believed that the earth was flat and that if you sailed far enough your boat would tip over an enormous precipice. It was believed for centuries that disease was spread as a consequence of wrongdoing, or the actions of demonic figures, or a disturbance of the four elements of earth, air, fire and water, or because of other reasons, until the dawn of modern medicine in the West gave rise to the understanding of the circulatory system, and the spread of infection.

You may smile at the thought of such ignorance, but maybe you need to think about what you believe to be "true", and the beliefs

The first problem for all of us,
men and women, is not to learn,
but to unlearn

Gloria Steinem

upon which you base your own life. You have begun to explore beliefs and expectations that limit your life. This chapter is going to focus on how you can loose the chains of ignorance, and develop a powerful understanding about your potential.

Living the life you love is something that you can all learn to do. But when you hear the words "learn" and "learning" something goes PING inside our heads, and you switch off! Learning sounds like hard work, it can make our heads ache, and you only remember lessons in school which were boring. And don't forget that boring teacher who managed to take the fizz from your best subject and make it as flat as two week old cola.

But learning need not be like that at all. Learning can be exciting, and fun, and hugely satisfying. Remember the day the stabiliser wheels were taken off your bike? How about the day you passed your driving test? Some people never forget the first time they learned to dive into a swimming pool, and others still get a kick out of the first time they stood up on ice skates.

We forget all the other skills we have learned that we now take completely for granted. Men can knot their tie in the dark; women can apply lipstick without a mirror; kids learn to tie shoelaces; babies learn to feed themselves.

In fact, if we made a list, we would discover that almost every skill that we take for granted had to be learned.

Here's one: sit somewhere comfortable, get relaxed, and fold your arms. There's no trick here. Just fold your arms comfortably and naturally. Now, fold your arms the other way! In other words, not right arm under your left, but the other way around.

If you have not tried this before, several things will happen. One - you think it's difficult to fold your arms "the other way". Two - when you do, it feels strange, and even a little uncomfortable. Three - you have to think - you are conscious of having to move your arms into a certain position, and when you have unfolded your arms and try to fold them the other way a second time, you still have to think about it.

We have, in reality, achieved mastery in the art of folding our arms through learning and habit.

The key insight about learning is this: you were not born with the life skills you take for granted. You learned them. They are not dependent on your DNA and genetic code. They do not depend on your parents or your upbringing or your circumstances. Research is discovering that you can learn almost anything you want to.

You can even learn to live the life you love, drawing on the skills and aptitude you have as human beings who are very good at learning, but have forgotten how to.

It is a mistake to think that the life that you love is "out there" and can be reached if and when you have enough money to pay the bills, get that particular job, lose those extra pounds from your waistline, or find your perfect partner.

Inner wisdom begins when you realise that you can learn to live lives that you love each and every day. You just have to start.

So - how can we learn how to learn, again?

Let's take an example you are all familiar with. It could be learning to drive a car, or bake a cake, or swim, or ride a pony, or tie your shoelaces, or touch type. But, let's take an example of learning which is not limited to men or women, geography or a particular age range.

Remember when you learned to ride a bike? At first you probably fell off more times than you can remember. Maybe there are a few scars to remind you But, you kept getting back on and starting again. And again. And again, until you progressed to that first, erratic wobble down the yard. "Hey, Dad, look at me" and then you fell off again! But you attained a level of success which allowed you to progress from wobbling dangerously, to riding confidently. You didn't have to think about it. And - before too long - you could even manage gears, take your hands off the handle bars and put your feet up in front of you. Riding a bike became as easy as, well, falling off it!

That was an example of successful learning. But sometimes - often - you attempt to learn something, and you do not succeed.

Take, for instance, learning a language. Remember the language tapes or CD you ordered so enthusiastically? Where are they now? And how fluent are you? Sorry to remind you about this, but you gave up.

Perhaps it was piano lessons?

Often, you do not learn as quickly as you anticipate. And you stop. However, all that effort was not unrewarded because you learned a lesson that you have never, ever forgotten, and it is a lesson that each and every one of us learned extremely well. It is this:

You learned how to give up

Strange as it may seem, learning to give up is something that you learned just as successfully as every other "life lesson" you have learned.

It doesn't take too long to realise that more or less every action you take, and every thought you have, is something that you have learned. And if you analyse learning a little further, you can begin to understand how you learn.

The Four Levels of Learning

Level One: awareness of what you can do, and who you can be.

This is when you first discover that what you can't do, or do not know and decide to do something about it. You are at level one when you see someone enter a swimming pool head first, rather than feet first, and learn what diving is all about. Level One behaviour means watching enviously as an elder sister rollerblades around the park, or when an uncle took you fishing, cast a fly on the far riverbank and asked if you would like to try. Level One behaviour was when you fantasised about your first car, and ached to have your first driving lesson.

In adulthood, in a work scenario, Level One behaviour is exhibited when you realise "I can do that" and apply for promotion, or when, in a leadership role, you look at your resumé and consider night classes, or business school, to enhance your career prospects.

In every case, Level One finds you on the brink of change, of being able to make a choice, or taking a decision. I am at Level One when I suddenly realise that something might, just might, be possible for me. I don't know if I can do it, or have it, but the possibility is there, and it excites me.

Mistakes are the portals of discovery

James Joyce

Level One and living the life you love

Everybody wants to be happy. Everyone wants to love the life they live. That desire and interest are powerful indications of a Level One experience.

Each of us is different, and the lives that we lead are different. But you have all experienced the Level One moment at different times. It could be the first romantic date. It might be your first visit to a foreign country. It could be the memories evoked by certain scents, or the recollection of a special moment.

The Level One experience is exciting because everything is possible. I can get that summer job and earn enough for me to backpack in Europe. I can ask that girl/man for a date and she/he will say "yes". I can be Chief Executive of my own company. I can have children. I can get that job. I can be President of the United States.

The Level One experience is profound, because at Level One you are at your most effective, most powerful, and most alive - in theory! You will be so articulate and impressive that you will get that summer job. You are so attractive that she/he can't possibly have an excuse to say "no"! You have the talent, the energy and the commercial acumen to be massively successful in business. It's you taking the oath of allegiance in Washington at the presidential inauguration.

Exercise:

I experience/d Level One when I:

    decided to win that scholarship

    chose to run in the London Marathon

decided to learn French.

When I....

When I....

Then - what happens next?

Level Two: clumsiness

Level Two is what happens! You experience Level Two when you lose your balance and fall off your bike. You suddenly realise that there is a gap between what you want to do, and what you actually achieve. Although you could imagine yourself riding your bike like your elder siblings, the reality is very different. And, falling off HURTS! You get bruised. You get cut. And - far, far more important - you look stupid. You get laughed at.

Remember the language cassettes you ordered? The excitement you felt as you worked through the first lesson? The commitment with which you decided to devote time to study?

And what happened? The first week was great. Well, almost great, because you did actually miss a lesson, but you intended to make it up over the weekend. And, what happened next? The commitment evaporated. Not because you were no longer interested in learning French - in fact, you may still want to even now - but it turned out to be more difficult than you thought. Let's leave the languages to linguists.

The slimming course and the gym subscription seemed such good ideas at the time. You had always wanted to be able to slip into that smaller size swimsuit: it was only a question of losing a few pounds. The slimming programme would do the trick. Just as the workouts at the gym were going to give you a six pack stomach. But, it didn't happen, did it? The slimming course wasn't completed, and the early morning workouts got squeezed out by lie-ins.

The value of Level Two learning

However, Level Two learning is a profound experience. Nearly every one of the setbacks you experience can be traced in some way to your Level Two voyage because you learned an incredibly important lesson. It is this:

You learn how to give up

That's right. Giving up is not something that just happens. Giving up is something we all learn to do.

Let's look more closely at this aspect of Level Two, because it is so important, and can be so valuable as you learn how to live the life you love.

How many of you have wanted to have a small business that you could run from home, alongside your day job? Perhaps you were attracted by a multi-level marketing company, or you had a practical plan for providing a c.v. service from home using your word processing skills. You moved from the Level One experience - visualising your success - to Level Two which is where you began to put your plan into action.

It is at this stage - whatever we are attempting - that we suddenly find we are clumsy. Not only is your plan more difficult than you expected, but you did not have the skills or perseverance required to succeed. You became frustrated. You got depressed. And you gave up.

We don't actually call it "giving up". We say we are taking "a commercial decision" or, "the market isn't ready for this idea", or "I discovered I wasn't good at languages".

31

The difference between Level One and Level Two

Level One is (generally) a mental activity. Level Two is (generally) practical.

Level One is always optimistic. Level Two is frustrating.

Level Two and living the life you love

The Level Two experience is what accounts for many people's cynicism about living incredibly joyous, fulfilled lives every moment of every day. "Oh - I tried that.. I read that.. I watched that.. it didn't work for me". In other words, you gave up on the idea that you could have an amazing life, or that an amazing life is actually possible!

Remember, you choose to stop doing something, to give up, for a reason. And the reason, generally, is that what you are attempting is "difficult" or "hurts". In other words, our pain button - either mental or physical - is pressed. You do not know how to handle the pain. And so you choose to avoid it. We all do.

Exercise:

I chose to give up when I

dropped out of evening class

didn't take up the full time job after a week's trial

stopped keyboard lessons

cancelled my fitness trainer

But you do not have to get stuck on this level, which leads us to

Level Three: I CAN do It!

This is the moment when "things come together". You can smoothly pull away from the kerbside in your car without embarrassing jolts; the cake comes out of the oven looking like a cake should look! Your tennis service lands the ball over the net enough times for spectators to turn to each other and say, "maybe I should get tennis coaching, too". This is when your fingers hit the right keys and you can (almost) touch type.

In other words, Level Three is when the hard work and perseverance of Level Two kicks in.

You still have to think about what you're doing, though. You have not got complete mastery - that comes later - and you still need to pay attention to the activity, but there is greater freedom and enjoyment. And as you practice your new-found skill, you become more confident, and this reinforces your ability.

Adults and Level Three learning

As adults, we tend to move relatively quickly from Level Two to Level Three, which makes the difference between the two levels hard to notice: the transition is often easier to observe in children.

Take a child learning to write, for example. At Level Two, the small fist grips the pencil tightly, the forehead is furrowed in concentration, the lips chew silently as each letter is carefully wrought on the page. The effort of writing for a child is - literally - physically and mentally exhausting. But, with practice comes accomplishment, and soon - with an inspiring teacher - the muscular tension transforms into an easy confidence.

33

One of the marks of adulthood is the ability to persevere in the face of the frustration you encounter in Level Two and to enjoy the freedom that accompanies Level Three activities.

We can identify Level Three activities in our leisure sports. Take golf, for example. Unless you are a golfing professional, each game requires concentration and attentive co-ordination. You can not take the putt for granted! If you enjoy more demanding sports, such as mountaineering, each stretch of a climb calls for focus and watchful application of knowledge and skill.

Level Three and living the life you love

You might think that Level Three would be a perfect place to spend your life.

Surprisingly, the answer is that it's a reasonably satisfactory place when it comes to doing things, but it is not so rewarding when it comes to being fully alive.

Why is this?

The answer lies in the way that each and every one of us achieves happiness.

We do so to the degree that we can make our lives our own. In other words, we are not dancing to someone else's tune

Learning is movement from moment to moment

Rainer Maria Rilke

(however attractive), or marching to another's drum (however seductive the rhythm), or paying lip service to creeds that do not have power and effectiveness in our lives.

Level Three living is characterised by the outward observance of social etiquette and convention which subtly conflict with your own inner beliefs.

So, for example, research shows that in national elections, few voters are actually influenced by party political broadcasts. You vote Republican/Democrat or Liberal/Conservative because you always have done/your parents do/your friends and peers do.

It is a truism that rebellious adolescents are also the most conventional: students organise demonstrations on campus during the day to demand freedom of thought yet have to meet the acceptable dress code of the peer group (fashionably correct trainers, logos etc.) in the evening.

Level Three living often highlights the contrast between outward signs of success with inner uncertainties. The high-flying executive with the external rewards of corporate life - car, perks, expense account and trophy wife - may well harbour increasing unease about the ethics of his commercial enterprise.

It is at Level Three that the cracks first appear in the happy facade presented by many relationships that are, in reality, far from happy. On the outside of a relationship, all may seem well, but within, two people can be increasingly unhappy yet delay talking about their feelings because of what "people" or their friends will think of them.

Level Three living is sometimes expressed like this:

"I go by what others tell me."

"We've always done it this way."

"We could do that but what will people say?"

"Is my bottom/nose too big?"

"I've never done that before."

"I know in theory it's the right/better/nicer thing to do, but....."

"Do you like this dress?"

And so on. When all's said and done, if you only live the life you love at Level Three, more is said than done!

Exercise:

I live at Level Three

when I nod my head in meetings but inwardly disagree.

when I got to Church/Synagogue/Mosque out of habit, rather than personal commitment.

when I go along with the crowd although I would prefer to do my own thing.

When I...

When I...

It might seem from all this that Level Three is "bad" or "wrong". Nothing could be further from the truth. Level Three living is an extremely effective stage of development for doing things. It is a necessary phase we go through, but it is not the best place to be for being fully alive!

The problem comes when we confuse doing with being.

Until now, we have not explored this amazing distinction between doing and being. You can do something extremely efficiently, yet be someone less than human. The Second World War concentration camps are an example of extremely effective murder systems designed and orchestrated by people whose humanity didn't reach the starting line.

But that is an extreme example. Here's another example that you can all identify with to highlight the difference between doing and being. Next time you are in the checkout queue at the supermarket, notice the shop assistant at the till. The manual dexterity required to handle your goods and move them past the bar code scanner is not necessarily of a high order, but it does call for speed and efficiency for every customer throughout that operative's work shift. But it is hardly surprising if the assistant has completely "switched off". In fact, if you say "Thank you" you are, understandably, often met with a blank stare before your comment registers.

Or, if you commute to work by car, consider this example of doing versus being Level Three activity. You will have done your car journey many, many times before. You know the route you take, the timing of the traffic lights, the awkward junction where the school bus collects children, the brief section of dual carriageway which allows you to drive slightly faster. You know this route, as they say, like the back of your hand.

In fact, you know it so well that when you close your car door you don't get into your car, you go into a trance! How many times have you arrived at your destination and wondered to yourself, "I don't remember driving here at all! I was on automatic".

There is a clear contrast between doing the driving, and being the driver.

Exercise:

I experience Level Three doing rather than being

> when I look at a television programme without watching it.

> when I eat cereal and read a magazine article at the same time.

> when I listen to a presentation and can't remember a single word of it.

> When I...

> When I...

> When I...

You can see that living at Level Three is practical, useful, and a way of life that works for much of the time. But it is not the whole story, because there is another level of living that you can experience, but which you often forget about.

It's time to find out about...

Some people will never learn anything, because they understand everything too soon

Alexander Pope

Level Four: The Life You Love

Level Four living is when being takes over from doing. Imagine you had entered the half-marathon. At 11 miles your legs would have ached, your lungs would have hurt and your arms would have felt like lead. But you would keep running. The thought of finishing within the time you set yourself (Level One) that spurred you to enter the race would keep you going. At 12 miles you might want to give up. You've had enough (Level Two). But you keep running, and when you stop concentrating on your legs pounding the pavement you realise you have covered another half-mile (Level Three).

There it is - the finishing line is in sight! You would suddenly experience a surge of energy and enthusiasm and everything comes together. Your stride lengthens, your breathing steadies, you are buoyed up by the encouraging shouts of onlookers, you feel gloriously, enthusiastically alive. The colours of the leaves, the sunlight bouncing off the tarmac, the bobbing colours of the runners' shirts in front of you, the scent of the spring blossom, and the lightness of movement comes that easily and consciously as you sprint the final 50 metres to finish the race.

That is what Level Four living is about: a mastery of being which allows you to be you because you have chosen to be so.

Let's take another example of Level Four living, one that nearly everybody has experienced.

Recall a moment in a relationship when you knew that you wanted to share your life with that special other person for always and for ever. It might be a romantic meal in a candlelit restaurant; it could be after a walk together on the beach at sunset when the clouds are salmon pink against the purple sea. Or it might be more prosaic: watching your partner walking towards you across the airport Arrivals lounge and being overcome with the blissful certainty of love.

At such moments, you can say whatever you feel, and know you will be listened to. You can hear whatever is said, and understand each and every word. Indeed, speech can seem immaterial because words suddenly become too weak to bear the weight of their meaning.

At such times, your workaday world is transformed. It is the same office routine, the same lunch break, the same sales meeting, the same crowded subway, but you feel completely different. In fact, colleagues notice that you're different. You have more energy, you are more relaxed - in short, you are blissfully happy.

And there are, of course, other moments: that holiday you spent scuba diving off the Florida Keys; the week you sailed around the Western Isles; the moment your first child was born; the day your team won the Cup.

Level Four living is when you live the life you love, and love the life you live.

It is not the strongest of the species that survive, nor is it the most intelligent, but the one most responsive to change

Charles Darwin

Exercise:

I experienced Level Four living when

I served two aces on the tennis court yesterday.

I finished the nineteenth century novel I wanted to read.

I wrote to my best friend at University who I haven't seen for 15 years.

When I ...

When I ...

When I ...

You've spent some time revisiting how you learn, and the stages of learning that you pass through. It might seem rather complicated, but that is only because you are taking a microscopic look at something that you are quite familiar with.

The key message is this: living a life you love won't just happen with a click of the fingers. Nor will you love the life you lead simply by "thinking" it. But all you need to do is begin learning how to live such a life.

———————

Question: I think I understand the difference between the four learning stages. But can the different levels co-exist alongside each other? Does it matter?

Answer: Of course. You can be a great tennis player, playing at Level Four and enjoying your game, and be a lousy cook operating at Level Two. Does it matter? No - unless you want to be a great cook! The great thing is, most of us operate at Level

Four in many different areas of our lives: computer keyboard skills, or getting the information we require, or parking our car. Any area of mastery in your life gives you a clue about the degree of excellence you can enjoy in other areas if you want.

Question: Is Level Four living something that is the absolute best. I mean, does playing tennis at Level Four mean you are a champion?

Answer: Well, it could do. Remember, Level Four living is when everything comes together. But, rather than being a series of isolated moments of "success" or "connectedness", Level Four implies a moment to moment continuity, and that can happen when you are typing, or clearing up after children, or walking along the street. There is a kind of total awareness that is without struggle or effort. Level Four is when you're most yourself, and fully alive.

Summary

There are four stepping stones of learning:

Deciding to learn (change)

Setbacks - learning to give up, unless motivated to.......

Stick with it

Mastery

Fourth afternoon

Thoughts for Women (... and others)

Here are some thoughts on living the life you love that are just for you.

For too long, women have had impossible demands made on them: perfect life partners, sexually attractive, nurturing, caring, wage earners, mothers. The list could be twice as long as this and still not be complete.

In many different cultures - and still, in many ways, in much of the West - a woman's own interests and needs have been put second to those of a man. Either as a daughter who has been side-tracked in favour of a brother, or as an adult whose career aspirations are secondary to her (male) partner; or as an achiever whose career is halted by an invisible glass ceiling, in contrast to the smooth upward elevator with "Men Only" engraved on the doors.

When it comes to living lives that they love, many women have naturally learned to be mistrustful, even cynical.

The pressure to conform to male stereotypes of sexual attraction is powerfully present in most developed cultures: the global

45

cosmetics industry preys on a woman's legitimate interest in looking good.

Women are far more prone to eating disorders than men; the woman's reproductive system means that you have to be wholly engaged in the consequences of unplanned pregnancy than a man.

And yet many women have developed qualities which allow them to live lives that they love far quicker than men who have lost their "feminine" strengths.

Women communicate their feelings more accurately and freely than many men; they are more emotionally integrated and less prone to compartmentalise their lives. Women often make better business team leaders, seem to have a greater ability to handle alternate views in meetings, and make balanced judgements.

All of which suggest that living the life you love will be easier for you than for many men!

Here is an insight that may be of value. Remember that the four stepping stones of learning, at this point, relate not to attempting to mimic male stereotypes, but to really examining what it takes to be fully alive as a woman, and what this means for you.

Exercise:

I like myself as a woman and feel a sense of inner power.

I have good friends of both genders.

I don't give my power away to men by automatically deferring to them by being submissive, or being defiant.

I express my intelligence and power openly when I am

with men, rather than hiding these strengths and expressing them in covert, manipulative ways.

I'm aware of put-downs women receive every day, but I refuse to let these alter my picture of myself.

I enjoy but avoid going over the top in my role as caretaker of others.

I enjoy and celebrate my sexuality.

I do not use my sexuality to manipulate others.

If I lived my life over again, I would enjoy being either a man or a woman.

I take care of my body.

How did it go? Did any of the statements above push a button?

The statements above are designed to give you an inkling of how you can make the life you love your life, not only as a human being, but as a woman too.

Exploring living the life you love as a woman

One suggestion that you might like to consider is to look at each of the statements above with your best friend. This person should be someone who you have shared secrets and gossip with, who knows you, and loves you. Someone you could go shopping with, who can tell you honestly that you look awful in those shoes, and you won't take it personally.

Why not set up a simple system so that you call one another at a set time every day for 10 days just to talk through together one of the above statements every day. Agree to be focused; only allow yourselves five minutes.

Lay down the ground rules beforehand so that both of you agree that there is no "right" or "wrong" about the conversation. Just take turns each day to start off the conversation beginning something like, "Well, for me, taking care of my body means...." and include examples of when you do, and when you don't do one of the above statements. Then share what it means to you, if anything (and, it may not).

The point is this: women are far more receptive than men to nurturing new ideas, letting them grow and develop and take them where they will. And women are far better than men - generally - at sharing honestly and in an uncomplicated, funny way, what is going on inside their heads and hearts.

What you are doing when you mull these ideas over is planting seeds in your inner garden that can develop and flower into powerful, beautiful plants that really express your whole self in an amazing way - naturally.

You simply have to let it happen.

Another simple exercise that you can do on your own is to think about the inner child within you. But on this occasion, think about the inner boy, not girl, within you. Consider the masculine side of yourself, the male side.

No one can make you feel inferior
without your consent

Eleanor Roosevelt

Maybe this is something that feels incredibly strange, alien, even weird, but when you allow your inner man to talk to you, you will experience an amazing wholeness and integration.

One way to do this is just to sit quietly when you are relaxed, perhaps after a shower, or when you are rested. Put on your favourite music, maybe sit in your favourite place, and have a sheet of paper and a pen nearby. (It is better to do this exercise with paper and pencil rather than sitting at the word processor).

Then, imagine that you were born not as a little girl, but as a baby boy. Imagine what you might have been called (perhaps you are aware that your parents always wanted a boy, not you?). Imagine yourself growing up - you go to school, you grow up, you date. You recall experiences that are important to you, but you gently see them not through your eyes, but through that boy's, or that adult man's eyes.

How would you have been different? How might you be different today if you were a man, and not a woman?

It is possible that you experience unexpected feelings while you are thinking about yourself as a man. Perhaps you feel envious, or angry, or resentful, or at ease, or excited - maybe ripples of each of those emotions, and more, wash through you. Just let them be, without getting upset or worried or judgmental.

Now, while you are relaxing in this exercise, being playful about it, ask yourself this question: as a woman, how would it be if I allowed the male part of me more room in my life?

Don't expect society's pressures to go away; they won't and, almost certainly, they will increase. What you can do, however, is to learn to live between the pressures, and enjoy your gender!

Fifth evening

How to Avoid Burnout - Vitality and Wellbeing

Stress and tiredness affect all of us. But it is possible to live lives that are filled with energy and vitality. There is a lesson to be learned from physical disharmony, and we can learn to live lives that are characterised by well being and health.

The concept of burnout comes from space rocket design, and refers to the point when the engine fails because it runs out of fuel.

In the same way, there comes a point of physical and emotional exhaustion when we as human beings "fail" because we do not have enough "fuel". Generally, we associate this breakdown with physical and mental symptoms, and someone who suffers burnout at work, or at home, can do so because of long-term stress and worry.

But, does this mean that you should lead lives where stress and worry are completely absent?

Common sense says that this would be impossible, and living the life you love does not necessarily mean that are days are spent in some kind of womb-like existence, protected from every unpleasantness.

So, why is it that some people succumb to illness and mental pressure, while others appear to thrive? What is burnout about?

This is where the four learning stepping stones contribute significantly to your understanding, because if burnout means anything, it means a stage where you have literally given up. Either your body exhibits signs of physical exhaustion, or your mind is so stressed out that you are incapable of making the simplest decision.

And you need to be careful of putting too much emphasis on a split between "body" and "mind" when you think of yourself. The reality that is "me" is infinitely more complex and sophisticated than can be explained by referring to two terms.

So, a key aspect of burnout is that it is less an energy failure - although those are the symptoms that we recognise late in the day - and more of a learning failure.

Burnout affects people engaged in worthy causes as well as those chasing corporate goals.

So, what is the learning that is not taking place?

This is the hardest lesson, but the simplest one. Burnout occurs because the way you are doing things, or the way you are approaching life, is not effective. In other words, the way you are

Every now and then go away, have
a little relaxation, for when you
come back to your work your
judgement will be surer

Michelangelo

approaching work or other situations is just not working, and your body, or your inner self, is giving you this simple message: STOP!

And, it is a message that all of us resist time and time again.

Sometimes, people resist so much that their bodies or minds "fail" just like the fuel exhausted rocket engine.

There are some, of course, who choose not to notice the warning signals, or even maintain that permanent tiredness is natural. You even hear it said in many corporate circles that if you are not tired, you probably are not contributing to the corporate mission. Such people wear their red-eye shuttle tags with pride!

Of course, if this is a matter of choice, then that is their responsibility. It would need to be done mindful of the knock-on effects of their irritability, short attention span and tendency to dominate others or their work colleagues or partners and families.

But, many people do not have that choice, and find that they are increasingly subject to pressures that take their toll on their peace of mind and emotional balance.

Well - that is how life is! You need to relax, let go of some of the resentment or hostility you may feel, and begin to take a mature look at your world. Rather than yearn for greener pastures which are always "out there" or in the future, how can you deal skilfully with your circumstances now so that burnout is avoided?

In other words, how can we move on from Level Two living, to Levels Three and Four?

As we have seen in earlier sections, the most helpful place - in fact, the only place - to start from is where you actually are, here and now. So, let's have a reality check about work:

Exercise:

I love my work and find it generally challenging and fulfilling

I'm paid adequately for my work.

If I could live my life several times, I'd choose the same work in at least one of them.

I keep a healthy balance between work and play in my life.

I know my work helps rather than hurts people.

The stresses and frustrations in my work don't hurt my mental or physical health.

If my work situation should conflict with my basic values, I would change jobs.

I don't lose sleep over work problems.

I don't frustrate others or myself by chronic "putting things off".

One of the symptoms of an approaching nervous breakdown is the belief that one's work is terribly important

Bertrand Russell

I don't feel I'm selling my soul to the "system".

I plan my work life as part of intentional career planning and goal setting.

And, here's a reality check about life outside work:

Exercise:

I find I have reserves of energy at the end of the day.

I've learned how to live every day as though I'm on holiday.

I am never rushed.

I don't jump red lights, and I let other cars in.

I don't miss things, or be late for appointments.

No one in my life thinks I should change.

People tell me - regularly - how well I look.

I treat everyone extremely well from checkout operator to partner.

I am at the centre of a very strong network of friends.

I don't have to prove myself.

I am at peace.

How did you do? And, remember, don't feel that your answers are right or wrong, or make them another, silent criticism of yourself.

The fact is, when it comes to burnout, everyone of us has to learn how to move from Level Two to Levels Three and Four.

So, how do we find the inner peace at the centre of the tornado? Or the calm at the centre of the storm?

The secret, of course, is not what you do, but how you are about things. Not doing more, but being more. One way to begin is to consider how you can be more mature about our daily life.

The fact is, at one level, most of us know what we need to do to sort out our day. It doesn't take a sophisticated software programme to work out a balance between sleep, the right diet, and appropriate relaxation.

But most of us find it very hard to put our good intentions into practice. This could be because we have forgotten how we learned to change; the more we give up our good intentions, though, the more we strengthen our ability to give up. After all, who do you remember best: the person you spoke to a moment ago, or the person you met last year?

We seem to learn best when there is a strong link between who we want to be, and what we want to do. This holds true even when we can't verbalise our thoughts: a baby learns to walk because even before she can talk, she understands that by

Our fatigue is often caused not by work but by worry, frustration and resentment

Dale Carnegie

walking she will experience greater freedom and, in adult terms, her full potential. Of course, there is parental motivation and encouragement, and we benefit from similar support as adults.

So, if you know, deep down, that your work is killing you, you need to start taking steps to sorting it out.

Does this happen easily? Not necessarily. Will it happen quickly? Not always. It can take years to stop wobbling on the pavement and cross the road to a lifestyle that really mirrors the person you are. But in the end, if it matters deeply to you, you will find that circumstances and events often combine to bring about situations whereby you can change and develop in the way that we want.

It may be that you genuinely don't know, or feel you can't see, the way forward from the dire situation you are in. You can feel stuck, or trapped by constraints and demands that you are not able to change.

Often, these constraints appear to be financial: I need this job to pay the childminder, to get the experience for where I want to go, to get the bonus that will allow me to start my own business.

You can learn to stop complaining, and learn to stop suffering, and learn to take responsibility for being where you are.

Who ran up the credit card bill? Who chose that particular house or flat, car, vacation, job, partner?

Look around! When it comes to choices, someone had to choose, and most of my choices were made by me!

Maturity comes when we can accept our choices - and when we do, burnout, stress, and exhaustion are suddenly less burdensome.

When you see that you chose to do certain things, you can see that there is the possibility that you can begin to choose alternatives.

Why choose burnout? Why choose stress? Why not start choosing vitality? Why not choose energy? Why not choose a life you love?

———————

Question: Aren't you being very judgmental about people who suffer stress at work? I mean, most organisations just pile on the pressure and make no allowances for individuals whatsoever. I don't see how someone in that situation "chooses" burnout.

Answer: Am I being judgmental? And how can someone in circumstances over which they appear to have no control be said to have any responsibility?

First, I have total sympathy with someone who is stressed out at work. But the way I can help is not to ask, "What are you doing about it?" but rather, "How are you being about it?" I'm not being judgmental but descriptive when I say that many, many people complain and don't do anything to begin exploring other ways of handling the circumstances they find themselves in.

So you do not necessarily have responsibility for your circumstances but you are generally responsible for your feelings about them.

Question: Are you suggesting that someone should put up with their lot and suffer in silence?

Answer: Absolutely not! I'm saying you need to learn to be incredibly compassionate and generous to yourself, and begin sorting things out, rather than delaying living the life you love.

Question: Can you say a little more about events and circumstances conspiring to help us change in the way we want? Are you talking about God?

Answer: I was being poetic, perhaps. But I wanted to open up the idea that when you find yourself "in the same mess" again and again, it might be because you haven't learned how to move on. In that way, the everyday circumstances you find yourself in are great teachers, because - in the end - you can start learning how to move on. If you're always in debt, for instance, it might take bankruptcy to give you the chance to start afresh. If you're made redundant from your job, however unsettling the prospects, it could be the chance to break away from a routine that is stifling you. If your relationship breaks down irretrievably, and you are faced with the bleak reality of separation from all that you hold dear, even your own children, it might still be the only way that you are able to move on to the next stage in your life.

Now - the interpretation or meaning you bring to these circumstances could be negative, "Things always turn out badly for me", or you could learn to "see" things differently. Sometimes, a religious tradition can give much insight in this area.

Summary

"Burnout" is a learning failure.

Handling "burnout" need not mean doing less, but being more.

We can learn to stop complaining, and learn to enjoy our responsibility.

Sixth Morning

A New Way of Seeing - Developing a Vision

Sophie put the glasses on.

"What do you see?"

"I see exactly the same as before, except that it's all red."

"That's because the glasses limit the way you see reality. Everything you see is part of the world around you, but how you see it is determined by the glasses you are wearing."

(From Sophie's World)

It can be very, very hard to take our glasses off! Most of us are wedded to the way we see life: our partners, our colleagues at work, our bodies, our children, our parents, even our very selves.

The way we see reality is shaped by our past experiences. When we were growing up, we learned that bees sting; that strong mustard can burn our tongue; that a candle flame burns; that too much chocolate (sometimes) will make us sick; that moving traffic is dangerous.

Whenever we encounter those "realities" again, we draw usefully on past learning experiences; and, of course, positive "strokes" also contribute to our sense of the world and its possibilities.

Just as we smile at teenagers rollerblading down the pavement, absorbed by the music playing through their earphones, we forget that we too have developed invisible earphones which we hear the world through. Like the teenager, we have forgotten we have them on. In fact, we probably wouldn't believe what we were hearing if we took them off!

Sometimes, however, what we thought was real might not have been the case.

When our parents shouted at us if they were harassed, we might have learned to equate raised voices with the slap on the back of our leg which always followed; soon, our "earphones" forget the origins of specific raised voices. We shortcut to equate any raised voices with pain, perhaps for no reason on our part.

How we hear things is a subtle affair. "You'll never be as good as your brother/sister/friend..." becomes: "I'm no good at anything...."

Or, "You're so stupid.." becomes, in time, "I am stupid..." with all the life consequences that you can imagine.

Sometimes, our "hearing" and "seeing" is defective, because of the invisible lenses and invisible earphones that we have learned to wear.

We are shaped and fashioned
by what we love

Goethe

"I'm fat/ugly/thin/spotty...." are often what we thought other people were saying, or thinking.

In a nightmarish kind of way over the years, the way we see and hear becomes a kaleidoscope of anxiety, insecurity, fear and uncertainty.

Sometimes we can recall vividly the moment when something was said, or the occasion when we did something that resulted in personal embarrassment, which we understand accounts for the way we feel about things now.

Often, however, we can't. Whatever happened, happened, and we coped with the consequences by - among other things - forgetting the exact words or situation. Which was probably for the best.

The effect of these invisible earphones and invisible lenses is profound, and makes up much of our conscious awareness about ourselves. Take any statement about yourself that you care to identify, and there the highest probability that it has roots and origins in our past.

In fact, the way we feel about our world is part of our personality, and part of what makes us attractive to others as well. Sometimes, people think that the winning trick in life consists of finding like-minded people who look at things (through the same lenses) and have the same ideas (listening through their invisible earphones as they do.

If we are surrounded by like-minded friends, however, there is a real danger that we will never have the opportunity to live lives that we love because our apprehensions and fears will be mirrored, and even reinforced.

How does all this relate to living the life that you love?

The way you look at life, and what you expect from it, depends entirely on your expectations. If you have learned to expect very little, if you have learned to become cynical, suspicious, doubting, hard hearted, cold, indifferent, intellectual, smart, hard, unforgiving or whatever - you have learned all these things, and got stuck. Because whatever comes to mind when you conceive living a life that you love will be because of the invisible lenses and invisible earphones that we have become so used to wearing that you have even forgotten that you have them on!

Remember the bicycle? When it comes to living the life that you love you have got stuck at the "falling off the bike" stage (Level Two) and decided that you were not going to go on learning. You gave up.

The way to get back onto that bike is to become aware of your invisible lenses and invisible earphones and consider - only consider - taking them off!

What will this be like? For some people, the change can be as dramatic as being blind, having an operation to have your sight restored, and awaking to discover that you can see all the colours of the rainbow. For others, it might be similar to discovering that you had gradually lost your hearing but due to revolutionary treatment you can now hear as well as you could as children.

*Before you attempt to set
things right, make sure you
see things right*

Blaine Lee

Birdsong, traffic, rain beating against the window, a cat's purr is as distinct and definitive as you can ever recall.

What would a new way of seeing and a new way of hearing be for you?

Exercise:

If I could "see" differently, I would be able to

Forgive my ex-wife

Learn a foreign language

Love my stepchild

If I could "hear" differently, I would be able to

Ask for that pay rise

Eat more healthily

Train for that fun run

The Four Levels of Learning and the ways we "see" and "hear"

We have looked at Levels One and Two above. So how do you move from Level Two (where you are now) to Level Three? In fact, how can you begin to even notice the spectacles and earphones that you have got so used to that they have become invisible?

First, start noticing when you get apprehensive, or upset, or when you don't want to do something.

Exercise:

I notice that I get apprehensive

> when I have to take faulty goods back to the store even though I am due a refund.

> when I have to telephone a stranger.

> when I want to discuss my career with my boss.

> When I...

> When I...

> When I...

You don't have to be overly introspective, or spend hours attempting to identify and exorcise in some way a precise moment in your past that contributed to the way you react to certain situations now.

All you need to do is to accept that in some way, somehow, something slowed you up, and you either didn't notice, or it was so upsetting that you did not know how to handle it, or learn from it.

The minute you begin to do what you want to do, it's a different kind of life

Buckminster Fuller

At that moment, your whole way of looking at life became subtly coloured - and you forgot that.

At such moments, you yield up your vision, and part of the joy of living a life that you love is not only re-gaining your vision, but holding the dream, and living it.

Here's how:

1. Accept that you are the person you are, and that you react to certain situations in a certain way, and that's OK.

2. Understand that whatever happened in the past happened for a reason which has worked well for you, but it does not have to shape your life for ever.

3. Consider different ways that you can handle situations that upset you. In other words, don't automatically go for the way you are "failing" to act now, as though that is the "only" or "right" way.

4. Write the following:

"I, _____ understand that my actual and inner vision may not be 20/20, and my actual and inner hearing may not be 100%. The way I see situations, make decisions and form opinions is probably flawed. I am not discouraged by this, and commit myself to be open to greater clarity as and whenever it presents itself."

5. Prepare to be surprised, intrigued, and energised by what you begin to "see" and "hear". Not only will you enjoy greater insight and effectiveness, but your vision of life will broaden and deepen.

Question: Do you think that I can develop a new way of seeing, or new vision, in an instant?

Answer: Learning to live without your invisible spectacles can take time; maybe less time if there is one over-riding "lens" through which you are looking at life. But, as you get better at learning, and enjoy it, the process is quicker.

But you can have a vision of what your life is about, or a vision of where you want to go, in an instant, and hold that vision from day to day as a kind of pilgrimage to where you are going. In fact, it's your vision that provides the "push" to learning to do without your invisible spectacles.

Question: How can I learn to act differently in certain social situations? I'm not particularly outgoing, and I don't really see myself as, or want to be, a loud extrovert. If I change, do I have to be different?

Answer: You don't have to change to see life differently. If anything, you have to learn to be more you. In other words, learn to rely less on your "spectacles" and more on your vision.

Question: Are you saying that the "lenses" that I see life through are all bad? If my parents were loving and kind, wouldn't that influence the way I see people for the better?

Answer: Absolutely. The way to discern the way that "lenses"' distort our vision is to notice situations where you feel uncomfortable or apprehensive. These are small clues to the past where your learning got blocked.

Summary

Our reality is shaped by our past experience

These moments - good and bad - often become like spectacles that we become unaware of.

However, these moments do not have to shape our lives for ever.

We can begin learning to improve our eyesight!

Seventh Morning

For Those in Their 20s and 30s (and beyond)

First, the good news: you have been given so much. It's been the same for every generation, but maybe the stakes are higher, more exciting, more rewarding, more exhilarating, and more scary for you.

In the West, your standard of living, your access to technological expertise, your ability to learn and keep on learning, the natural optimism of hope, and the raw energy of intellectual ingenuity allow you dominate the workplace of the future in a way that is wholly different from the past.

You're part of the information age - you're probably wired into it - and the opportunities for travel and your interest in spiritual values have never been greater. Your independence and indifference to "how things are done around here" allow you to develop solutions on your own initiative.

You are able to live with "blurred vision" in a way that your parents were never able to. Conventional values are less certain, careers more fluid - certainly less stereotyped - alternative lifestyles proliferate, and a commitment to a personal relationship can be delayed until.......whenever?

And now the other side of the coin: it's going to be tough. Much is going to be asked of you. You can't afford to stop learning; you're going to need to continuously learn and develop. No job is safe anymore. With less security, it's harder to make personal sacrifices for other people.

It's never too early to consciously begin to live the life you love. This means that you have begin now to nurture your vision, and hold to your dream. Don't dilute your idealism. Do not be seduced by artifice. Trust your intuition and instincts.

How can you do this?

At this stage in your life, you want to notice the direction and movement you are taking along life's river. If you want to know how things are going to turn out in the future, take a moment to reflect on how things are going now. This is not a question of outward success or change, such as professional qualifications, or having/not having a career/relationship(s), or status. It is to do with your inner direction.

Become interested in moving away from meeting expectations. Question the degree to which you are living the life you love, or one that has been designed for you by (well-meaning) parents, or your social group.

Become interested in moving away from facades. It isn't easy to shift from the crowd, from your clique, until you experience a closer, richer definition of who you are.

Become interested in moving away from pleasing others. So often (and rightly) we have defined ourselves by pleasing others (parents, teachers, employers etc) rather than defining yourself by what you feel, in your heart's core, to be authentic for you. Begin achieving this now, and you will have a lifetime's satisfaction, in spite of its turbulence, ahead of you.

Become interested in moving away from "shoulds" and "oughts" and "musts".

When you start "moving away", you are - using the analogy of the river - moving away from the river bank, the shallows, the rocks, into the faster flowing, deeper water, which will carry you further and faster to where you want to go.

You are moving towards profound autonomy and self-direction, towards becoming all of the complexity of your changing self; towards trusting yourself - and others.

In this period of your life, you have the opportunity to become the person you really are; someone who can love, and who will be loved. When you look back on this stage of your river, you'll realise that it started here, and that the journey was worth it.

Eighth Evening

Anger and Depression

Anger and depression are part of life's mosaic.

We can learn strategies to cope effectively when we feel paralysed.

We need to understand how anger and depression contribute to our inner growth.

Dark nights of despair will pass.

It happens, doesn't it? Everything goes swimmingly for a couple of days, a week, maybe longer, then - wham! - something happens and it is as if those good intentions, actions and approaches were as out of date as an 80s computer.

When this happens, and it does, there are two directions you can take. One is to be absolutely thrown off balance. When this happens, whatever you are attempting to do or change: kick a habit, learn a new skill, take more exercise, you give up completely. It is as though the activity or task has become so scalding hot that you decide never to pick it up again.

Generally, you emerge from this process feeling better about yourself, determined not to make that mistake again, and often derisory about the activity.

Or, rather than give up on the activity, you give up on yourself, and get angry, sad and depressed. "I'll never learn/finish/achieve/master....." while elevating the activity to Mount Everest proportions of unattainability.

In both instances, unless something happens to shift your thinking and behaviour, you will remain stuck at Level Two learning, having chosen (in this case, not learned) to give up.

And, often, we actually wallow in this frame of mind, like basking hippopotamuses in warm mud, feeling sorry for ourselves, angry about the situation, helpless, and playing two internal music cassettes labelled, "Poor Me" and "Isn't it Awful?"

Does this matter? Are we weak and stupid when this happens? Not at all! Why do we do it? Because, generally, we haven't learned a strategy or skills that shift us from this sticky, gluey morass.

Then what can we do?

One of the first things that we need to do (and this always seems easy until you are actually in this situation!) is to relax, relax, relax.

When we are uptight, angry, fed up and a roaring furnace within ourselves, our whole bodies are tense. On other occasions, we can feel physically exhausted, and unable to carry out the

The only thing that has to be done today is breathe

Michael Angier

simplest tasks. Even getting out of bed seems a waste of time and energy. ("What difference will it make?") In this case our tension is so strong that it paralyses us.

So how do we shift ourselves out of this state to how we want to be?

The first step (and these are small steps - shuffles, if you prefer) is not to take your mood too seriously. In other words, don't confuse the feelings you have with the real you.

Next, don't worry that your vision and values are in ruins. They are not. Really, they are not. OK, so things have not gone the way you expected, but there is probably something that will be of value that you can learn.

Then ask yourself, "How will this look in two weeks/two years/10/20 years' time?" The answer, probably, is that it will not be significant at all. Honestly, few things matter, and most things don't matter at all.

Again, if you have these thoughts of failure and lack of self-esteem (and, on these occasions, these thoughts buzz inside your head like flies around a refuse bin) try and do something humorous: hum a tune to yourself, hop around the room, or sing out loud. If you're alone in a car - shout as loud as you can. Really yell out loud! Go on, LOUDER!!!

Then, even if lethargy and torpor seem to cling to you like seaweed, just do the small things that need doing. It is amazing, and irritatingly surprising, what a difference small actions and activity make in shifting your mood from one of bleak despair to a realistic understanding of the situation.

Go for a short walk, wash the dishes, pick three weeds from the window box, clean the computer screen, empty the waste paper bin.

When you do this, you shift the focus of your attention away from yourself and your preoccupations and onto something else. And this is one of the keys to embracing a life that you love.

The fact is, you are not super-human. Honestly, you're not. You are a normal human being with all manner of demands and expectations placed on you by others. You have ideals and dreams and goals that matter deeply to you. And, some days simply do not go the way you expect or want. It has nothing to do with you, but the mistake you make is to think that, somehow, you are responsible for what happens.

You're not. At rock bottom, the only thing that you are responsible for is how you are being about the situation, not the situation itself. Our job is to be fully human and fully alive, and anything less takes away from everything that matters to us.

So what you can do is to begin to develop plans for when things go wrong. Develop your own Disaster Scenario. Most people don't. They live every day as though it is going to be perfect, and are then completely thrown off balance when circumstances take them by surprise.

But imagine an airport that did not have contingency planning for a power failure or a major incident? Would you like to be held up in a 10-mile motor car tailback knowing that the highway services did not have any plans for diverting traffic?

The cure to anger is delay

Seneca

It is not negative thinking to develop personal disaster plans. It is not saying that life is bad and that everything is awful. On the contrary, it is recognising that, generally, life goes on just as it does, but that I am the one who does not handle the situation well because I haven't planned or thought about how to manage if it changes.

Let's take some simple examples. How about the journey to work?

If you have a 50 minute car journey to your office, you can spend every minute that you are delayed in a tail back cursing and blaming other drivers. Or, you can accept the delay as a fact of life, and adopt alternative strategies for handling the situation such as leaving earlier, or buying music tapes you really enjoy.

Here is another example: a boring business meeting.

It is very tempting to mentally snooze through a business meeting. Look around the table and see how many people are doodling, surreptitiously updating their diaries, or scribbling notes to their neighbour. You can join in, or you can be different. One tactic is to actively check whether you are needed; if you are, decide beforehand to participate as fully as possible. Read the briefing papers beforehand, rather than once the meeting has begun. Ask questions. Take notes. Absorb yourself in the present moment. In other words, you can't change the situation, but you can change how you are being about it.

A more complex example of a personal disaster scenario is when we really lose our temper. It may be out of character for us to vent our feelings massively; we may be right; we may be wholly wrong. But what has been said, has been said. Someone will be hurt and upset. It would be easy to storm off and do nothing more. But a little forethought can still allow the situation to occur, but for you to be different afterwards. How? You can apologise.

81

Four ways to apologise when you've blown it:

1. Face the music and apologise in person.

It's tough, it's humbling, and it hurts. But if you're sincere, it often leads to a real shift of relationships. You'll be respected.

2. Apologise by letter or email.

You can choose exactly the right words, re-write it several times until you say exactly what needs to be said. Don't expect a response, and don't refer to it afterwards.

3. Apologise by telephone.

You might want to draft a "script" so that you go through with it and don't get derailed if the other person isn't in and you get an answering machine. Be straightforward, honest, and brief.

4. Apologise by mending fences.

If you broke it, spilled something on it, scratched it, or smashed it, see whether you can replace it. If you can't, a gift accompanied by an apology might be best.

When you apologise, you put the past into the past, and allow the other person to do so. If you don't, what was said or done festers

There is no birth of consciousness
without pain

Carl Jung

and rankles, both in your head, and the other person's. When the past is settled, you can enjoy the present moment, and that's what living the life we love is about.

However, there are times when we are just burdened inwardly. At moments like these, enjoying the present moment seems moonshine. When we're depressed, it can take forever to do even the simplest activities. (We're not talking here about clinical depression, by the way, which requires skilled professional and often pharmaceutical assistance. Check with your doctor.)

In our age, depression is a psychological, physical and spiritual condition that we are hugely ill-equipped to deal with effectively. When we get to the bottom of the curve, it seems that it will never end. In fact, depression can truly be described as the dark night of the soul.

Such "darkness" is well documented by poets, holy women and men of many different religious traditions, as well as writers and thinkers. Unfortunately, many of their insights are, to a large extent, lost or inaccessible for people today, and all we have in their place is bare medical knowledge.

This is similar to trying to figure out a magnificent work of art by asking a paint technologist! She may be accurate, but will not necessarily see the whole picture.

83

The dark night of the soul is often described by words like "abandonment", "losing your way", "helplessness", "feeling worthless" or "utter despair".

These phrases, and others like them, mirror one thing: a fundamental loss of value. Either your own esteem, or sense of another's value. In spiritual terms, this can be understood as losing sight of God; in contemporary language, depression can point to a complete lack of meaning in your life, where there are no values to give it meaning.

When you feel you are in the middle of this dark night, you feel that there is no certainty, no peace of mind, or no sense of purpose. In short, you can see no value in life.

It seems to me that this dark night is a necessary part of growth. Wise guides in the past have drawn comparisons with periods of transition found in nature: the way that a chrysalis changes into a butterfly, or how a snake sloughs off its skin. But however poetically and beautifully the dark night is expressed, the reality is that it hurts, it hurts, and it hurts.

From our first days in primary school we are trained to think, to enquire, to be curious, and to learn. We make choices, we develop opinions, we know what we think about our world. This is how we navigate through life. But then, in the dark night, all this security vanishes. It becomes a real struggle to make sense of every moment of every day.

What, then, can be the value behind this real depression and suffering that it seems we are all called upon to experience at some time or another?

Perhaps it is this: every one of us can delay, but not thwart, learning lessons of experience throughout life. While the lessons may be different for each of us, the process is the same. The pain - the dark night - occurs when we have to let go of our comfortable notions, ideas, attitudes, mindset and outlook in order to move forward and be receptive and benefit from what comes next.

And the more you resist, the tougher it becomes, and the darker the night.

But - and this may have to be taken on trust - as you are able to let go, you let go of what is stopping you from being most truly yourself.

Loving the life that you live can seem impossible when you are in the throes of the dark night of depression, or buffeted by the storms of inner anger. But you can learn to understand that these moods and feelings are part of your inner landscape, but not the whole geography. You can learn to plan ahead, and to accept that you may have to let go of what makes sense to us in order to grow more fully yourself.

That is what it may take to become fully alive, but it's worth it.

———————————

Question: Are you saying that I shouldn't see a doctor, but stick things out if I am feeling seriously depressed?

Answer: Not at all. The point is this: if you are worn out, exhausted, and unravelled by the trials of life, you need every assistance you can find, including medication and therapy if they are appropriate. But you also need to realise that you are not "bad" or "weak" or less effective as adult human beings because you are suffering in this way. On the contrary, your suffering may well be a signpost for others who, paradoxically, can't allow themselves to feel pain.

———————————

Summary

1. We can learn not to be thrown off course by anger and depression.

2. We can learn strategies to cope effectively when we feel paralysed.

3. We need to understand how anger and depression contribute to our inner growth.

4. Dark nights of despair will pass.

Ninth Morning

Questions for Men (.....and others)

Research suggests that while women are better at "parallel tasking" (being able to juggle different activities) men are more capable of single focused activity. This has tremendous value, but some drawbacks too.

The main disadvantage is that someone who is highly effective at focusing on end results tends to assume that the goal counts for everything. Sometimes, however, growth in wisdom and emotional stature comes from being able to live with questions without rushing to the first answer.

One of the issues facing men in a developed economy relates to work and success, the way that they manage day-to-day living, and how they grow and develop as people.

The reason that many men find that they lead lives of quiet desperation within corporate gilded cages, rather than lives that they love, is because - being goal focused - they moved quickly from Level Two to Level Four in terms of career, problem solving, and maybe even choosing a marriage partner.

When this happens, however, short term gain becomes long term pain. Part of the learning process lies in living within some questions, rather than rushing like an express train towards an answer.

89

When you live within a question, you allow yourself the space to consider several options. Within this space, you can remain free from quick judgements, and a sense of right or wrong, or good and bad, or success and failure.

The following questions are not designed to have quick answers, but to give you a chance to reflect, and ponder, and consider freely where you are, and what it might take to live a life that you love.

Section A

Business and career success

Are you in a career or profession that is totally fulfilling?

How well do you manage people? How do you know?

Have you reached a level of mastery in your career?

Do you enjoy being highly professional, or is it an effort?

If you had total financial security for the rest of your life, what would you do?

Be yourself. Who else is better qualified?

Frank Giblin

Section B

Day-to-day living

How well do you accept praise?

How do you behave when things are really tough?

Do you hold grudges?

If your life were a business, how profitable would you be?

Is there a rigid boundary between work and home and recreation?

Are you honest?

Are you living in the past? The present? The future? Problems? Aims?

What frightens you?

Do you know your weaknesses well?

Do you have enough money in the bank not to worry?

Do you put up with a lot?

Section C

Growing and developing as a person

Are you happy with how you look?

How do you feel about your body?

Are you confident?

Are you a loving person?

Are you happy?

Are you cynical?

Are you at peace with yourself?

Are you a sensual person?

How open are you to new ideas? Really?

What are you known for?

Section D

Living the life you love

Can you give and receive?

Do you have goals or pipe dreams?

What is your intuition like?

Are you deeply in touch with your family, and wider family?

Where are you in your life?

How good is your ability to learn?

Are you a spiritual person?

Do you have enough love in your life?

Notice the thoughts that go through you when you read these questions, and how your body reacts. There will be some questions that provoke a gut reaction, and others that you feel wholly at ease about.

The important experience to give yourself is not to rush to a yes/no situation. Really give yourself space to "dwell" in questions, particularly those that you notice evoke an uncertain response.

One way to learn to do this is to take one particular question and make it your question for a whole day, or a week. Write the question in your personal organiser, or if you have a private workspace you could turn it into a screen saver on your computer. Find a simple way of reminding yourself of it. Just have that question in your mind and don't try to come up with an answer in a hurry.

You will find that the question begins to give you something. It may well seem that you can't get away from answering, (that's an indication of how powerful your answer-seeking skills are) but gradually you will find that the question gives you a measure of freedom.

So, for example, "Where are you in life" might have elicited a quick mental response, "X years, X job, X children". After a little while, however, you might find an easing-up which allows a less clear cut answer such as, "I'm not sure" without any accompanying feelings of failure. Then you may find that you have "space" to begin reflecting more deeply on different opportunities that are available. Until now they have been squeezed from your thinking.

For many men, the greatest shift available to living lives that they love is moving from instinctively describing themselves in terms of what they do, and to begin exploring and deepening their lives in terms of who they are.

Tenth Afternoon

Discover the Power of Meditation

Meditation is not difficult: you can learn to meditate without learning strange mantras or sitting in uncomfortable positions. The benefits are enormous, and the long term value for living a life that you love is beyond calculation.

By now you will have discovered that living the life you love has much to do with how you think about your life, and how you approach each and every situation.

You can approach things unthinkingly, and react without any reflection, or you can stop yourself and say inwardly, "A-ha!" and notice which learning stepping stone you are standing on, and whether it is the right place to be.

Wouldn't it be marvellous if you could develop that awareness so that it was almost natural, that you were always at Level Four? The answer is that you can, and the way is to learn to meditate, and to make meditation part of the life that you love.

At this point, it might be helpful to take a few moments to notice your reactions to the words "meditation" and "meditate" and see what they mean for you, and what reactions you have to them.

95

Exercise:

When I think of the word meditate

I think of incense and joss sticks.

I think of chanting.

I think of sitting painfully cross legged.

I think of.........

I think of ....

I think of ....

I think of ....

When I think of the word meditation

I think of boredom

I think of self-centredness

I think of silence

I think of ....

I think of ....

I think of ....

Of course, meditation can be all of those things, so don't be surprised at your feelings. Just recognise that they were probably the right ones to have when you had them, but they might not be the right ones now.

Meditation is often associated with particular religious traditions - often Buddhism - but it is also a technique for enhancing the life you live that has been an integral part of western thinking.

There is not going to come a time when you wake up every day and say, "Yes - I'm living the life I love!" Part of that process is learning to make it happen, and meditation is the fast track button that will allow you to do so.

When you meditate, you gradually and enjoyably learn to manage the way you approach life and think about what happens to you.

We are all beginners, and often, when practising a skill like meditation, beginners bring more insight and clarity than "experts" who may have slipped into habits that don't help.

So, what is meditation?

Meditation is very special momentary time.

It is special, because it is a period that you give to yourself that isn't like other moments when you are alone, such as driving, or commuting, or sitting at a computer terminal.

It is momentary time, because when you meditate, you experience the quality of life from moment to moment in a way that allows you to understand what it means to live the life that you love in other parts of your day.

Stressed executives find a few minutes meditation before a meeting allows them to regain a sense of balance and perspective. Busy parents discover that meditation provides an oasis of calm in the middle of hectic activity. Students find that meditation aids their ability to concentrate and recall information, and reduces exam nerves. There are numerous health reports that underscore the beneficial effects of meditation on such conditions as blood pressure, hypertension and a range of emotional upsets.

A description of meditation

One meditation teacher has famously described meditation as "bringing the mind home". When we "bring the mind home" we recognise that much of the time we are not living in the present moment: our thoughts and our "selves" are often far away.

"I'm sorry, I wasn't thinking...I was miles away...I was daydreaming...I was thinking of something else...". You probably use phrases such as these many times each day. Add up the number of times that you do so each week, and then each year, and over a lifetime you could be alarmed how often you do not actually live in the present moment.

When we bring the mind home, we finally integrate and link up our whole being, which is what living lives that we love is all about. Meditation is the place and time that we can practise doing so, without having to step outside our front door.

Meditation is like an aircraft simulator where pilots can learn to fly complicated and expensive aircraft - even crash them - without leaving the ground. You can make mistakes, you can try something over and over.

The quieter you become, the more you can hear

Babb Ramdass

This is why you often hear the phrase, "practising meditation", because meditation is not something that we "do". Meditation is an activity we practise and what we practise is not "doing" but "being".

In this sense, meditation can be accurately described as a life simulator, because when we meditate, we experience every single emotion and feeling that we experience outside meditation time.

Anger ... envy ... greed ... sexual desire ... jealousy ... peace ... calm ... anxiety ... tiredness ... boredom ... happiness ... discomfort ... itching ... "pins and needles" ... irritability ... frustration ... depression ... sadness ... tearfulness ... grief ... compassion. You can see that there is no end to what we can experience every day of our life.

Meditation provides a safe environment for you to be yourself, and in being yourself, to experience these moments for what they are - just moments. And then, to notice that when you experience these moments outside your meditation period, that you can bring to your life a completely different response.

And that is when you start living the life that you love, and loving the life you live: when you can smile and see that it is not to do with having more, but being different.

Meditation is the bridge that allows you to walk over to that way of life that you have only dreamed about until now.

So, how do you begin to practise meditation?

Like every significant personal development experience, there are meditation "experts" and many of them have something of value to say. However, ask a software engineer how the Internet works and you may be watching your coffee cool for some time.

Talk to a graphics designer about a particular advertising campaign, or a retailer about store design. People who know lots about their particular subject tend not to be able to answer a query in a simple and straightforward way.

It is the same with meditation. Subscribe to any world wide web-based discussion group, and you will be amazed at the intricate, technical discussions aroused by the simple question - how do I learn to meditate?

It would be quite understandable if you were immediately put off and think to yourself "that isn't for me. I obviously have to understand psychology and yoga and it all sounds rather weird!" But the reality of meditation is totally different, just as the experience of a lazy weekend by the beach is different from the hurly-burly of the rush hour to work.

Living the life you love takes place in time, and the quality of those moments has something (often, quite a lot) to do with the quality of the lives you lead.

At one level, it is like jogging. How do you start jogging? Well, just do it! Meditation is the same, and while there are many useful books on meditation, and there is a list of them at the end of this book, you can link learning how to experience meditation to the four learning stepping stones.

All miseries derive from not being able to sit quietly in a room alone

Blaise Pascal

Stepping stone one and meditation

First, let's just pause for a moment and think about these words, "total" and "momentary" and "time", to begin to understand the richness of what is in store for us.

The American Heritage Dictionary of the English Language defines "total" in this way: complete; utter; absolute.

When you look up the word "time" you read that it is: an interval separating two points on this continuum; a duration.

So when you put meditation under your microscope, you can find that this single word is packed with exciting meaning and potential:

An interval separating two points on this continuum that has a high degree of excellence that is absolute.

And, if you put that into everyday language, what do you find?

Total Momentary Time (also known as meditation) is

A period of time that is absolutely wonderful.

So, you find yourself at Level One learning, not knowing, perhaps, what meditation is, and yet have a mental awareness that you can describe to someone else, even if you can't experience it yourself - yet.

Of course, this is not to say that there are not other periods of time that matter a great deal. We can all relate "a period of time that is absolutely wonderful" to other experiences: making love, a fantastic piece of music, or a particular holiday.

What meditation does is make these other periods more frequent: it is like oil that lubricates an automobile engine, or software that improves the efficiency and effectiveness of our personal computer.

There is no reason at all - other than your own wariness - for each and every day not to be made up of time that is absolutely wonderful. Practising moments of meditation will allow you to do just that, and learn how to make them more and more of our lives.

Level Two and Meditation

Level Two living, remember, is when we actually practise a skill, behaviour or approach to living. With that in mind, let's now practise meditation.

First, while you can meditate anywhere: in an airport departure lounge, in an elevator, in the car in stationary traffic, it is probably best to begin simply in your own apartment or at home.

Time of day: choose a time of day that works for you, but be realistic and appreciate that you will probably have to make time for meditation at first, and something else will have to be shifted around. Most people find that the morning is best, because they are tired out at the end of the day, but it could be that your schedule works best to organise your meditation in the evening after you have showered or unwound.

If the doors of perception were cleansed, everything would appear as it is, infinite

William Blake

However, you don't want to practise meditation just after a meal when your blood sugar could be altered and you feel sleepy, nor should you practise meditation if you have had alcohol or any other mood altering substance.

How long? Start with 10 minutes. Of course, you may want to practise for a bit longer, but like any new activity, give yourself space and freedom to experiment. Many people find that it is helpful to set a kitchen timer to the amount of time they want to meditate, so that they do not get distracted.

Environment: make the room or corner of the room where you are going to start tidy enough so that you don't get distracted by clutter. Switch on the telephone answering machine and turn down the volume or simply unplug it. Switch off your computer, TV or radio. You do not have to draw curtains and create a mysterious atmosphere. However, if the sunlight is very bright you may want to adjust the dazzle factor by pulling down the blind.

If you live in a shared house, use whatever conventions you have - a closed door, for example, or a sticky note - to indicate that you do not want to be disturbed. That way, again, you won't squirm with apprehension if someone arrives back early just when you are comfortable.

You may find that you would like something near at hand to rest your gaze on - a vase of flowers, a plant, a candle, a stick of incense, a picture of Jesus, Mary, Buddha, or your special spiritual guide. Equally, you may not; there are different meditation techniques, but many suggest gently closing your eyes during this time, so you do not actually need anything to look at.

However, what almost every teacher and advisor recommends is the way you sit. Most of us are familiar with the cross legged, or Lotus position, but this does not come naturally to many westerners, and it is not a position that you have to sit in order to experience the amazing value of meditation.

What is important is that you sit so that your spine is straight - a soft sofa or armchair doesn't work. As in everything, however, try it out for yourself; you will discover the value of sitting comfortably, with a straight back, not in a tense way, feeling your head balancing restfully on your shoulders.

Your hands can rest on your knees or thighs; gently close your eyes, and sit peaceably, calmly and normally.

At first, you may notice all manner of thoughts in your mind, cascading like a mountain stream down a steep hillside: that's fine; in fact, those thoughts - whatever they are - are absolutely normal.

But after a few minutes, you might notice that the thoughts are less like a fast flowing mountain stream and more like a slower flowing, broader river. It could be that you are quieter in yourself. You may notice that your breathing is different.

Take a moment to notice your breathing. As soon as you do, of course, your chest will tighten and your heart will pound. Just go on breathing in and out, in and out, in and out.

Heaven is a palace with many doors, and each may enter in his own way

Hindu saying

Try keeping your eyes closed - not screwed up tight, nor heavy lidded as if you are dropping of to sleep - but closed gently. This takes some getting used to, because most of us close our eyes only to sleep. In the context of meditation, we close our eyes to become fully awake.

Don't worry about your thoughts: just let them come and go. Don't get caught up in an internal dialogue, or when you do, simply let it cease.

One way to let the inner voices grow calm is to allow just one voice to be present: your own. As you breathe in, mentally "say" the words, "in-breath"; then, as you gently exhale, mentally say to yourself, "out-breath". Just keep gently breathing in and out.

There are many claims made for meditation, and research increasingly demonstrates its beneficial effects on our body and mind. But this does not mean that you should expect them immediately, or that they will be the same for you. It will be surprising if they are not present, but generally, when we learn to do something, we are too concerned with the question, "Am I doing this right?" or, "Am I good enough?".

So, Level Two finds you practising the experience of meditation. As you know, it is at Level Two that you often learn to give up what you are doing, and it is often the case with this activity too. Many people go on pilgrimages to foreign countries or spend weekends in exotic locations with a special teacher in order to learn how to meditate, yet find that after a few days on their return the effect disappears, and they do not keep a simple routine in place.

What can be done to establish the foundations of a regular meditation period?

There are simple habits that will help.

Try to stick to the same time each day, but don't impose a schedule that becomes a burden. It may be better to sit and practise five days a week, and not force the weekends when it is difficult. Better to have a schedule that pulls you forward, than a tyrannical timetable that pushes so that you are not able to keep up.

Try and stick to the same room, or place in a room. Over 2000 years ago, Aristotle noted that excellence is a habit: you simply have to develop a way of doing things that becomes natural, though at first it will seem strange, and may conflict with our usual routine.

Stick to the same length of time, and don't worry if nothing seems to happen. If you don't feel anything, if you get crotchety, if you are suddenly overwhelmed with angry or hurtful thoughts about someone or a work situation, just accept them as part of your meditation time.

The point is, there is nothing to think, nothing to feel, nothing to expect, no way to behave, and no particular thoughts to be thinking.

What you are doing is allowing yourself time - or rather, moments of time - when you are absolutely yourself. This is time when you allow your quality, and your excellence - what is most you - full rein.

And you have to practise to do this. Believe it or not, it will take practise. Not a lot, but on a regular basis.

This is how you will shift imperceptibly from Level Two to Level Three.

Level Three and Meditation

Here, you are not having to think so much about what you are doing. You have learned not to be surprised that you have apparently day dreamed for an entire 10 minute period.

It is important, perhaps, to become aware of all the ideas and thoughts that surround the word "meditation". If you have been brought up within a specific religious tradition - Jewish, Christian, or Islam - the word will conjure up memories from the past.

If you have become interested in personal development, maybe even been on some kind of retreat that centred on Asian or Eastern religious insight, such as Buddhism, then there will also be memories connected with that.

Here are some examples of what I mean:

> I feel funny about meditation because...

> It means sitting still for ages and that's boring

> I'll have to sit cross legged and it hurts

> I'll have to sit cross legged and I can't

> It's got something to do with incense and

> I don't like the smell

and so on. The point is this: just become aware of any thoughts that may be putting you off the idea of meditating, and gently put them on one side. Remember what you have learned about giving up: you became stuck at a certain point in learning an activity or developing a skill, and lost sight of your goal.

Let's look again at some of the possibilities that might become available to us when you practise meditation:

I'll have far less stress and hassle

I'll feel calmer and more confident

I'll have more energy

my sex life will improve

I'll make friends easily

I will get more done every day

Why does meditation contribute to our lives in such amazing ways? The answer is - we're still finding out. There are significant research studies that monitor the heart rate of someone while they are mediating, and measure the electrical activity of their brain, and check "before" and "after" attitudes.

What seems to be the case is that meditation is good for you - really good - and, like fresh vegetables and healthy a diet, you can do with lots of it. But, like a change in diet, if you approach it in an over-serious, heavy fashion, the chances are that you will not really give it a fair chance.

But, you can find out for yourself! So let's make a start...

Most people, however, find that meditation creates more time than it takes

Peter McWilliams

There is a great advantage in practising meditation in the same place. It is this: you will develop a real ability to meditate anywhere. You will be able to quickly "slot into" your meditative frame of mind because of the associations of, say, a picture or a candle or incense stick that you use when you meditate.

What you will discover is that your meditation becomes a space that expands into your whole day. Rather than finding that your meditation period of, perhaps, 20 minutes is just a one-off, you will discover that you are able to "come from" your meditation at every moment of your day if you choose to. That is one reason why so many people value meditation so highly.

For example, if your working life is extremely stressful - deadlines to meet, difficult colleagues, demanding children - and you manage to develop a frame work which allows you to practise meditation regularly, you will be able to draw on that meditation period at other points in your day.

If you are in a difficult meeting and want to make a controversial point but are afraid of saying what people won't want to hear, you will be able to draw on your meditation period. When you do so, you will find a reserve of personal confidence that gives you enough edge to contribute in the way you want.

If you are driving and someone cuts in ahead of you, or pulls across dangerously, rather than involuntarily cursing them and counter-driving aggressively, you will notice that you will be calmer, and less quick to react angrily.

If you feel totally drained and exhausted when you leave the office, and dread the crowded, jostling commute back home, you will find that you are able to relax really deeply, even in the midst of pressing strangers and cramped travelling because of your meditation.

Remember, you are only learning to practise meditation. That is why you can relax and just let it happen. When you practise something, you don't worry if you make mistakes, drop the ball or miss the serve. It's all part of the learning curve.

The only thing you need to aim for is sitting like a rock. That's it. Don't worry about your thoughts. Don't worry whether you are doing it right. Don't worry about whether you should be feeling anything. Just sit like a rock. Steady. Firm. Grounded.

And, allow yourself to be your own meditation master. Of course there are moments when you will benefit from a "coach" - every activity does - but believe me, you know far more about meditation than you think.

You can get help from a spiritual guide, but you now have access to a myriad of information sources from which your understanding of meditation can develop: books, tapes, videos, short retreat centres and, of course, the Internet.

Rather than starting from the point that you know nothing about meditation, why not consider that you know a great deal? This is not arrogance, simply a statement of fact. Most of us do know far more than we give ourselves credit for, and this applies to meditation as well as to everything else in our life.

Imagine you had to give a five minute instruction on meditation. You could do it, brilliantly. Of course, there might be a question that you don't know the answer to, but that's OK. When you lead a life that you love, you're allowed to say, "I don't know the answer to that question, but I'll find out"

There are some practical points that you need to bear in mind when starting to practise meditation.

First, and you have come across this elsewhere in this book, do not rely on your feelings to decide whether you want to meditate or not.

It's not that your feelings don't matter - they do - but none of us are very good at discerning what our feelings are telling us. If we are feeling tired, it is more likely that your feelings are reporting physical sensations about the late night we had, rather than your thoughts about meditation.

If you have that "I can't be bothered" feeling, it is more likely that your feelings are reflecting your general downbeat sense, rather than a specific reluctance about meditation.

Practise meditation whether you feel like it or not. There is something different about your meditation when you have had to actively choose, rather than meditate on the crest of a "Hey - this is great!" euphoria. Don't ask me to explain this, but wait for it to happen. It will, I promise.

Next, another tried and tested principle that people who have practised meditation for some time agree on is that it makes a difference if you have a routine, or habit. It may be twice a day, it may be once a day, you may meditate every other day, but find a pattern that works for you, and stick at it!

Notice the word, "pattern", rather than "habit". Quite reasonably, we often have a question mark over habits as they carry suggestions of routine and mindlessness about them. A pattern, on the other hand, conveys more strongly the idea of expectancy. This sense that meditation is an expected part of you day is what counts. And for a reason.

You may not have ever lived by the sea, and it is possible that you have never had the chance to spend a day on the seashore, and noticed the tide coming up the beach. Slowly, little by little, it creeps up the sand. Gradually, the bay or estuary fills completely, and the tide is full. And then, inexorably, the water recedes, the waves lap their way down the sand, exposing seaweed and shingle at the lowest point of the tide. And so it goes on, day in, day out, year after year, for millennia.

The point is this. It is not the fact the tide rises and falls - the tide's habit - but what happens below the water's surface. This is the real value of tidal water. Ask any marine biologist what happens on the seabed as the rising tide brings food and nutrients to the fish, crabs, and tiny barnacles who cling to rocks. And that is only when the tide rises!

There is a parallel with our meditation. It is not the repetitive pattern that matters; it is what meditation makes happen below the surface of your life that counts.. And we need this nurturing, energising, cleansing "inner tide" on a regular basis.

Some meditation techniques you can practise.

Every athlete, painter, musician and professional of any kind practises. This is what keeps them moving towards Level Four in their chosen profession. Sometimes the practise they take is intricate: a keyboard player will practise complex chords; a drummer will practise over and over until he is satisfied he has the rhythm exactly right; world class athletes have to train for hours every day.

Sometimes, however, their practise is pretty simple: scales, gentle jogging, relaxed games against friendly opponents.

Often, books about meditation stress complicated techniques to do with breathing or visualisation that puts you off. These meditation techniques are simple, and enjoyable; and you can use them for ever.

The pebble in a pool meditation

This is a very simple, peaceful, calm technique that you can practise any time, but is best begun during meditation moments.

After you have begun meditating, as suggested earlier in this section, begin to gently repeat these phrases to yourself:

"May I be happy. May I be peaceful. May I have serenity."

Now this is the hard part: go on gently repeating these phrases. Don't worry if your attention wanders, you will be able to bring it back gently to where you are. Just keep on softly murmuring the phrases: "May I be happy. May I be peaceful. May I have serenity."

You do not have to murmur the words aloud. You can think them to yourself; it doesn't matter; just keep the gentle momentum going: "May I be happy. May I be peaceful. May I have serenity."

Gradually, you will begin to feel a sense of meaning to the phrases that you may not have been aware of, but this is not a thinking exercise; just accept that the power behind the words is doing its work - like the tide - in the rock pools of our heart. Just keep on gently repeating the phrases to yourself; "May I be happy. May I be peaceful. May I have serenity."

Then, when it seems right for you, change the phrases slightly:

113

"May my friends be happy. May they be peaceful. May they have serenity."

Notice what is happening? Like the expanding ripples on the surface of the pool after a pebble is dropped in, your meditation is widening to include others. When you do this, you are learning to expand your heart, and allowing your natural reservoirs of love to flow outwards to others.

You can make further ripples:

"May my family be happy. May they be peaceful. May they have serenity."

"May those who may have harmed me be happy. May they be peaceful. May they have serenity."

Don't worry if you find that thoughts about work, or plans for the weekend distract you. The attractiveness of the meditation technique I have outlined here is that you can use these "distracting" thoughts as part of your meditation.

So, if you suddenly find yourself thinking about someone at work (who you may not like particularly), you can simply include them in your meditation: "May he (or she) be happy..peaceful.. serenity." You will probably find that this is a more effective technique than trying to empty your mind of thoughts, and banishing distractions.

Here is another meditation technique.

If you have been brought up within a religious tradition, and have a devotion to a particular saint or holy person, you might want to practise this next meditation.

First, arrange things so that you are sitting in a comfortable position and won't have any distractions, as suggested earlier.

Then, begin to imagine that your special saint, holy person or religious figure is present with you, meditating with you. Allow yourself to feel the incredible kindness and love that this person feels for you, and for all. You might visualise the room being filled with a warm light, and your being surrounded and part of this amazing compassionate love. Allow yourself to enter into this circle of love.

Then, you could begin to acknowledge this person and say gently, "Mary.." or "Buddha", or "Jesus.." or "Father.." or your holy person's name. Just gently breathe their name, or quietly become aware of their presence. Allow your meditation, perhaps, to be guided by them, accepting that whatever and whoever comes into your mind will be part of their love too.

This technique is especially helpful when you are feeling tired, have a low energy level and just don't feel you have the strength to even sit still for one minute. Rather than do it all yourself, allow your meditation to be "carried" by this other, special, person or being.

Here is a third meditation technique that will make a difference at certain moments when you may have been knocked off balance by bad news, or want to really help someone who is physically distant from you.

How often have you felt frustrated because you have heard that a close friend of yours has had really bad luck - slipped and broken a bone, or a long relationship has ended, or they have lost their job - and you may have spoken briefly but want to do more?

How often have you felt powerless to do anything in the face of appalling news of some human disaster in another part of the country, or elsewhere in the world?

The following meditation practice provides a technique where by you can make a difference. Here's how.

First, get yourself sitting in your meditation position, either in a chair with a firm back, or kneeling back comfortably, or sitting cross legged. Either way, remember to keep your back straight.

After a few minutes spent centering yourself, let any anxieties or distractions melt into the background and notice your breathing.

This is the difficult part. Just notice your breathing. Notice each breath as it comes into your body, and notice as it goes out. In, and out. In, and out. Don't hyperventilate; just notice the in-breath, and then the out-breath.

Then, call to mind the situation or person you feel deeply about. It could be a famine area, it might be a relative taking important exams; maybe there is a friend who has suffered a bereavement; perhaps someone you know well has had a serious financial setback.

Just take a moment to recall that person, or the event. Do not analyse the situation, and don't get sucked into problem solving, just hold the situation in your awareness.

In this state of awareness, breathe in gently, and go on breathing out. Then, as you breathe in, breathe in the despair or fear or anxiety of the situation, and breath out calm, or compassion, or forgiveness, or love - whatever you feel is the appropriate emotion. It may be that you do not really know, and can just trust your intuition and inner wisdom.

This is an extremely powerful meditative technique, but it is quite demanding as well. You need to be very relaxed about your breathing, and you also need to have a certain amount of concentration so that your mind neither wanders, but remains gently focused on your intention, nor do you get uptight or frustrated with yourself when you attention wanders - it will!

Tension is who you think you should be, relaxation is who you are

Chinese Proverb

And it requires a deep trust that "all will be well, and all manner of things will be well".

Trust is at the heart of meditation. Trust - even when you have no evidence because of your feelings or thoughts - that what you are doing is of value, either to yourself, or for others.

You will find, however, that your life regains a balance and energy so that when you are not able to find time during the day to meditate, you notice the difference. It is not the end of the world, but you will be able to start practising again.

And that is all there is to it: Trust and practice. Just practise. You will be able to be quite light about this, and not serious. Don't make a big deal out of your meditation. Just laugh it off if people tease you; they might at first because that's what we do when our friends get interested in something new that seems strange to us. But the ribbing ceases when your "new" interest becomes part of your everyday life. In other words, as you move from levels two and three to level four behaviour living.

Question: I find it really hard to sit still even for 10 minutes! I get so distracted. Do you have any suggestions?

Answer: Is it the sitting still, or the distractions that seem to get in the way? If you have problems with sitting, it may be that you would find it helpful to get some help and make sure that you are sitting as comfortably as possible. And, it can take time to get used to. As far as distractions go, don't worry! They'll always be there. They don't matter: you will learn not be distracted by the distractions.

Question: I like the idea of meditation, and have found it really helpful sometimes, but then during the rest of the day the period of quiet seems so far away. Any ideas?

Answer: The secret might be to think of your meditation period as your own personal sprinkler system which releases water throughout the day. You might find it helpful to have 'taps' that you can turn on. Put a small sticker near your computer screen with 'M' on it, in a favourite colour that will remind you of meditation. Just glancing at it will allow you to "turn on" your meditation "tap".

———————————————

Summary

Meditation is something everyone can learn.

You do not have to sit in an uncomfortable posture.

You can practise meditation anywhere.

You can't make any mistakes when you meditate.

Allow yourself to move with the meditation tides in your life.

Eleventh Morning

How am I Doing?

Have there been any issues so far that you think are significant?

Have you noticed any change in yourself about things you used to take for granted?

Are you finding that situations which seemed fixed are not so immovable?

Have you practised any meditation? What was it like?

There are various approaches to living the life you love. Some people bring brute force and effort, and make martyrs of themselves (and are horrible to be around) when they diet, or take up jogging, or whatever they feel will transform things.

As you can see, this book adopts a different approach, and suggests strategies based around the way we learn. Every so often, as on any journey, it is helpful to stand back, take a breath, and check that we are still going in the direction we want.

So, this morning is designed to be a change of pace and mood: time to relax, and loosen up!

That is one purpose of this morning's work, but it is also to open up an extra dimension of living to the full.

It is this: none of us exists in a vacuum. We are part of a larger group. It may be that you are in a relationship, but if you have a job, you are part of a work environment. If you work from home, then you have another network of relationships. And those social webs are themselves part of a wider framework. We are all interconnected. It can be an unusual but rewarding exercise to work out exactly how large a community we belong to, and how intimately we are related to one another.

After all, if you meet a stranger it rarely takes long to find that there is some point of contact that neither of you would have believed was possible. Perhaps you discover that you have a mutual friend or acquaintance; sometimes it is a college or university, for others, army units or service corps is the connection. Maybe it is a shared enthusiasm for a popular soap programme on television, or a pop group; others prefer opera or art. Or it could be a hobby or interest.

You need to take this into account when learning how to live the life you love. It is not a question of retreating into a golden cage and blocking out anything or anyone who you don't like. In fact, it is the opposite: a fulfilling, authentic life actually has enormous space to allow people and circumstances in.

This exercise is to begin remembering how we fit into a wider picture, and how that picture includes us.

It is solved by walking

Saint Augustine

Exercise - The web of life

Find a large piece of paper - the bigger, the better. A piece of flip chart paper is ideal, but you can do this exercise in a notebook; you just have to write smaller!

Start by drawing a small circle in the centre of the page, and write your initial in it. Then draw another circle alongside, which might be your family, or work. Join the two circles with a line. Then, draw lines to other circles that link to each, and additional ones that you add.

Before long, your page - even the largest one - will be an intricate web of interconnected circles representing your whole life. It can be as detailed or general as you like, but you will find this an absorbing and relaxing exercise that reminds you how you are linked in so many different ways, and part of a larger picture. Your web of life is rather like a family tree, except that it is lateral rather than vertical.

The fact that you are part of a larger picture also has implications for the life that you lead, in terms of balance.

123

We begin our lives wholly dependent on others. As babies we would die if we were abandoned. Part of growing to maturity is learning to grow apart and, literally and metaphorically, learning to stand on our own two feet.

But a key component of a life that is hugely satisfying is also discovering the balance between being part of a social web, and being independent. Many of us tend either to be more isolated than we would like to be, or unable to spend time on our own because we don't like our own company.

For example, many professional people not yet in a stable relationship cannot entertain the thought of being alone at home one evening a week. They feel they have to be out partying or meeting friends. In contrast, young married couples or single parents can feel they are trapped in their homes with young children and never go out.

Similarly, many organisations have created what were thought to be friendly open plan work areas but are finding that people lack the privacy to think quietly. On the other hand, there is none so isolated as the senior executive who finds that her internal e-mail has been curtailed and recognises it as a not-so-subtle sign that she is about to be fired.

Traditionally, people have been categorised into two psychological "types": introvert and extrovert. These are often misunderstood words, because they are very precise terms used in traditional psychoanalysis, but they have entered everyday conversation to describe "people who prefer to be by themselves" (introvert) and "people who prefer spend more of their time with others" (extrovert).

If you lead a frenetic life that leaves you exhausted at the end of each day, you need to explore strategies that will let you spend more time which is devoted to "you", rather than being caught up and losing yourself in activity. Equally, if your work demands that you spend much of your time on our own, you will need to build in time when you get away from the computer screen and enjoy other people's company.

When you're finished changing,
you're finished

Benjamin Franklin

Exercise:

What's my mosaic?

We're all like a mosaic, lots of brightly coloured, attractive small stones that fit together to make a complete picture. Every picture is different - that is the glory of individuality - but we all share the same, basic "stuff" of life, our DNA code, our "human being-ness". Every mosaic is as good as the other, but some can be grouped together, and others form another collection.

It is helpful to confirm your hunches in this "people" area. Because living the life you lead includes other people, and often the main reason why you feel that you aren't living a great life is either because you are with the wrong person (relationship), or the wrong people (work, family).

Exercise: If only. . . . .

I would be able to live the life I love:

if only I wasn't having to care for my parents

if only I didn't have to work

if only I had a different job

Equally, you can feel frustrated because you are not with the people you would like to be with: another person (in a satisfying relationship) or another group (job/family/etc.)

I would be able to live the life I love

if only I was in a different relationship

if I was able to acknowledge my sexuality

If I lived somewhere else

If I...

If I...

Wisdom lies in learning to strike a balance that works for you between being with others in a way that is enjoyable (work, social relaxation) and having time to enjoy your own energy (working out, jogging etc).

Do not be too quick to jump to conclusions and immediately cringe at the thought of joining a Salsa dance class or taking up tapestry. It can be that you have learned to allow yourself to become lazy, and taken an easy option which means that you cut yourself off from so many options in life.

Let's look at what this means in terms of the four levels of learning:

Level One: as young children we are far more flexible and socially adaptable than we can probably recall: babies love exploring, and finding out about their world on their own; equally, they enjoy a close bond with their parents, and siblings.

This is how it happens. We get the Dream, but we don't get to dictate every step towards the dream

Peter McWilliams

Level Two: within our circumstances, we learn to make choices, and choose to be more outgoing, or to prefer time on our own. Most of us remain at Level Two, and get stuck. But we don't know that. We think, "This is who I am......"

When we feel are not enjoying the life we love, it is generally because we are stuck at Level Two: we have given up on the opportunity and possibility of life being different.

When we allow ourselves to move to Levels Three and Four, without necessarily knowing exactly what that will mean, we begin to open ourselves to living the life that we love.

Question: I found doing the Web of Life exercise quite hard, because I realise that I don't feel close to my family at all. Does it matter?

Answer: There may be very good reasons why you have moved away from your family emotionally. So, at one level, it does not matter at all. However, if you feel regret, or have a sense that you would like the relationship to be different, then you have a choice. Things can go on as they are, or you can consider some alternatives. But the initiative will almost certainly have to come from you. And don't expect members of your family to move as quickly as you might have done. Remember, they have learned to think about you in a certain way too.

Question: How can I do something, or commit to something, without knowing exactly what it will mean?

Answer: Without meaning to, we often put restrictions on our life. We make rules as to how things should turn out. So - "We'll go to the beach if it is sunny" is quite sensible. But, "I'll love you so long as you are nice to me" is less reasonable. We often block off whole avenues of possible outcomes, and deny ourselves the fullness of lives that we love, because of these conditions that we set for ourselves. So when we begin something without knowing exactly how it will turn out, we are opening ourselves to a far wider spectrum of opportunity than if we say to ourselves, "It has to be just so..." for us to enjoy something.

———————————

Summary

The point of today is to learn to relax, and allow the life you live to happen! After all, it is happening right now all around you. All you have to do is begin to see it for yourself in its entirely, which includes others, as well as yourself.

How relaxed do you feel about being part of a group?

Are you at ease spending time on your own?

Have you done your Web of Life exercise?

Allow your own wisdom to flow when you meditate.

Twelfth evening

Sorting Out the Mess - Coping with Breakdowns, Addictions and Disabilities

> At the end of this section you will have a clearer idea about
> what you can change and what you can't. Living a life you
> love does not mean living in a garden of Eden where there
> aren't ravenous tigers and poisonous snakes; it is possible to
> learn a completely different and empowering approach to
> serious upsets in your life.

Things happen. Water pipes burst. Your car gets vandalised. You
get ill. Your friend's sister is raped. Innocent hostages are
murdered. Your brother/sister takes drugs.

People do horrible things to one another and, sometimes, to you
too. You get victimised at work. You get mugged in the street. You
are involved in a life-threatening automobile smash through no
fault of our own. You test HIV positive. You get cancer. You lose
a vital faculty. And, you die.

There are countless strategies for coping with personal disasters.
For many, a religious tradition is the first and surest refuge in
times of crisis. The solace afforded by the sacred scriptures or
holy texts of the great faiths provides help and relief when well-
meaning words fail to ease heartache and pain.

Others choose an alternative approach. Their answer to horrible
events is to cut themselves off and pretend it isn't happening.

Denial of reality goes some way towards coping with terrible calamity and misfortune. And, in a way, it mirrors what our bodies do in the face of sudden trauma . We black out: nature's way of reducing psychic trauma in the face of impossible pain or injury.

Another group of people faced with grotesque injustice and evil choose an activist, angry approach. Their solution is not to accept passively the bullying tactics of a political regime, local gang or ruthless multinational. They organise direct confrontation, and fight like with like.

The problem is that most of us aren't like that. We are not the heroes and heroines who will go down in history for initiating great changes. As a consequence, we get depressed about what we see around us. And we feel helpless. "What's the point? There's nothing I can do."

132

This provides the key that will unlock a door out of the room of suffering and pain. Generally, you have to learn to do less, and to be different. The more you understand this lesson, the more you will find that you love your life.

Look at Level One awareness in this area. This is where to start: you discover that things happen in life that you don't understand which really upset you.

We are healed of our suffering only
by experiencing it to the full

Marcel Proust

Level Two awareness is where we learn to hold certain opinions about the way the world works:

"There's nothing that can be done.."

"If your time is up, your time is up..."

"There's a bullet with your name on it..."

"The world is a horrible place.."

"There's no justice.."

"It's fate..."

These opinions become fixed, yet they do not provide help or support.

Level Three awareness is when we struggle to "make sense" of what is going on. This is hard work, and yet it is worth sticking with it, because when we do so, not only are we able to live at peace with ourselves, but we are also able to contribute to others, either if asked, or by understanding where they are.

Level Four awareness is a deep, humble understanding of the grandeur of our world, with both its beauty and dark sides. Level Four neither assumes that there are questions with satisfactory answers, nor adopts a superficial quick-fix with no respect for the enormity of grief, pain and suffering.

You see, when you live the life you love, it also requires you to love the life that we are all living. And it is this life with all its mess, genocide, cruelty and spilled blood. Because that is reality. This is the world, warts and all, that we live in. We even carry it around in our very bodies at a microscopic level: cells multiply and die; infection ravages our immune system before we take an antibiotic. For a brief moment, in terms of geological time, we keep these marauding forces at bay, until we too become part of the greater scheme of things, and die.

There will continue to be injustice, murder, rape and genocide but there may yet be a time when our planet is utterly different.

But when you "love" this life that you live, it does not mean that you approve, or understand. "Loving the life you live" means that you accept life with all its imperfections without having to understand; you are realistic about your capacity to influence events; and you are committed wherever and whenever possible to being different in the face of negativity and evil.

Today's teaching: If we are to bring about change, we need to begin with ourselves.

Less of "Why don't they do something?" but "How can I behave in a different way about this?"

Generally, this means giving up looking for answers. Stop pretending that there is a magic key that is going to unlock all this stuff about "good" and "evil" and that you can wait until you find it before anything changes for you.

Begin letting go of the idea that there is a reason, or that there is a "purpose", or "God's plan" or "Allah's wisdom" or karma.

We don't see things as they are.
We see them as we are

Anais Nin

Begin afresh. Cultivate a beginner's mind when you read about tragedies in the newspapers, or learn about the sudden death of a close friend. Start remembering what you've forgotten. Rather than remain floundering at Level Two, where you will be stuck as long as you search for meaning or reason in the face of wretched unhappiness, cultivate a beginner's mind.

This fresh outlook will not happen overnight. Remember, you're having to undo many years of thinking and behaving in a certain way. Just like moving into a new house, it will feel different. In fact, it will be different because you are!

At first, you will fall unthinkingly into familiar patterns of speech and agreement. A pal will stop you in the passageway and begin telling a joke that you realise is risqué. You may join in the laughter as readily as you did before, but feel uneasy. Gradually you will learn more effective strategies because other people will notice that you are different.

135

On another occasion, a girlfriend might e-mail you the latest gossip about a friend you both know. Before, you might have eagerly pressed "Reply" and returned a bitchy comment. This time, you might simply press "Delete" and continue with your agenda.

Rather than joining in the clichéd denigrations about a political figure, or foreign leader, you might choose to remain silent.

And, you can practise in front of the mirror saying, "I don't know"; "I don't have the answers"; "I don't have the information".

Remember, moving from Level One Awareness to Level Two is a process of information gathering.

When it comes to personal upsets, there is only one piece of information that has any validity. It is this: "It happens."

Rather than cursing and swearing when someone drives badly and scratches the wing of your car, take a breath: "It happens".

When you read of a disaster that claims the lives of schoolchildren: "it happens".

Does this mean you don't care? Not at all: you care enough to read the article, watch the news programme and not turn the page or switch channels.

But what you don't do is start unspooling the "isn't it awful?" cassette.

What are the benefits? Less stress. Less despair. Less worry. And less anxiety.

The move from Level Two Awareness to Level Three requires action. You need to think and speak differently (or not speak at all) and this takes practice.

But we're all beginners at this, and one of the notions we have to give up is that both the world and I should be perfect.

One of the joys of living the life you love is that you do not have to be perfect.

We are continually faced by great opportunities brilliantly disguised as insoluble problems

Lee Iococca

A common thread that runs through any discussion or upset or setback or disaster is this: it shouldn't have happened because my idea of perfectionism has been wrecked.

In other words, setbacks and disasters serve a real purpose because they confront your assumptions about how life works. And that is such an important insight.

Situation:	**Assumption:**
It shouldn't have rained	I need perfect weather
Why did s/he get cancer?	I ought to understand
Why am I fat/thin/ugly/not the way I want?	I should be different
Why does s/he drink?	There must be a reason
Why is my child handicapped?	It shouldn't happen to me
Why does God allow suffering?	God is dysfunctional
Why is there hunger?	There is a magic wand...
And so on...	And so forth...

The fact is, most of our assumptions and opinions are of no value at all because they don't help. Assumptions and opinions are wishful thinking centred on your own, fractured view of your world. Most of us are like walking onions with layer upon layer of opinions and assumptions about the way the world should be.

So, wipe your eyes, and begin de-layering yourself. As you do - and it doesn't happen overnight - you begin moving from Level Two Awareness to Level Three, with some slipping and sliding in between.

Level Three awareness, remember, is still wobbly, but less so. You have mastered that art of balance and just need practice. And letting go of your assumptions and opinions is an art, not a crude, sweeping gesture. (Of course, some assumptions do seem to have validity: if it is raining outside, I will almost certainly get wet if I do not wear a raincoat. In these instances, they explain phenomena that tie in with your experience, not what I think may/may not/should/should not happen.)

Sometimes you can find the wobbly balance almost unbearable. You cling to the desire to make sense of your world. Does this mean that the world is meaningless? That there is just no point in living?

No. But you are near the centre of the problem here, and nearer still to Level Four Awareness. There probably isn't any organised meaning to what happens in life, other than the meaning you choose to bring to it.

The only meaning that you can be certain of is what you can see, and taste, and touch, and hear. In other words, what is happening in reality. Because "happening" happens. In other words, "It happens". And, that's all there is. That's all. Not Good. Not Bad. Not Right. Not Wrong. Not Awful or Godawful. These things happen.

Once you really begin to experience the liberation of that insight, the tension surrounding the situations and circumstances in which you find yourself begin to loosen their grip, lighten their hold, and disappear.

Question: Can you say a little bit more about not being perfect? Surely we all ought to try and become better people. Aren't you being really negative?

A nswer: We need to understand more fully the difference between being truthful, and being perfect. When we are truth-full, we allow our real selves to flow; when we try to be perfect, we are probably attempting to meet someone else's idea of what we should be. For many of us, being "perfect" is a source of anxiety and stress. As you learn to live the life you love, however, you will discover that "perfection" isn't something in the future; in fact, the present moment is absolutely perfect, whatever is happening in your life.

Summary

Things happen to us that we don't like.

Some terrible things happen on our planet that we cannot comprehend.

We can learn to handle setbacks differently.

We can learn to question our assumptions about what is "right" and "wrong" and "awful".

We can bring less meaning to our life without feeling meaningless about it.

Thirteenth afternoon

Money and Freedom

> Money is THE issue in our lives. We can be financial
> prisoners, and can see no way out of our dungeon. But we
> can relate differently towards money, and live a life we love
> through our mature relationship with money.

When you throw a stone into the water, it finds the quickest way
to the bottom of the pond. It's exactly the same with money.
Every thought we have about it goes straight to the centre of our
heart. We feel good about what we earn; we feel bad about how
little we possess; we worry about how much we owe; we panic
about being poor; we're exhilarated when we have an
unexpected windfall.

Often, our body reactions are linked to our thoughts about
money: a curt letter from the bank manager can send our
stomach into spasm; the unblinking numbers on an automatic
cash dispenser showing how little money we have in our account
can make our heart pound.

For many people, living the life they love is intimately bound up
with the amount of money they possess. National lotteries
conjure up dreams of the way that your life will be transformed
if you win the jackpot; magazines build their circulation with

photographs and envious stories of rich (and therefore happy) people; it is almost as if money has an overpowering scent that acts like a powerful narcotic. It attracts you with its allure, but it always leaves you wanting more.

If you are to lead a life you love, however, you need to begin to unravel all these thoughts about money. As you do so, you will discover that - in itself - money is not good, or bad, the source of ultimate happiness or the source of all evil. Like everything else, it is the meaning you give to that gives it power over us.

Let's begin by starting to look at one scenario that is very familiar.

Exercise: Debt, Money and Spending

A=Always S=Some of the time H=Hardly ever

My credit card balance is always near the maximum borrowing limit	A S H
I have little or no savings	A S H
I know I can borrow from someone when money is tight	A S H
I have a stack of unopened bills	A S H
When my pay slip or welfare money arrives I feel an overwhelming sense of relief	A S H
I deliberately write cheques that I know will not deliver	A S H
I hate talking about money	A S H
I am frequently short of money	A S H

How many As, Ss and Hs did you get? And how do you feel if you have a cluster of As? Do you feel depressed? Do you feel a failure? Angry? Frightened?

Remember, how you feel about money is often how you feel about your life. And when you experience those upsetting, negative feelings, that is often exactly how you feel about your life.

Allow yourself to feel differently about money. Here is another checklist, but this time it is centred on money within the context of the life that you love. Your statements about money could look like this:

Exercise:

Money is just one part of my life.

My income is increasing 15% a year.

My taxes are paid on time and professionally organised.

I have no hang-ups about money.

I have a regular savings plan:- at least 15% of what I earn, every month.

I have all the insurance and retirement plans that I need.

I understand savings and investment plans, and have the ones I need.

I give 10% of what I make in tithes, time or cash to those I love.

I have £150,000 in savings or cash account that I can draw upon.

Just imagine how you would feel if every one of those statements were true for you: wouldn't you be loving the life that you love?

Or, would you?

143

How about this exercise. Consider these statements:

I always have everything I need.

My debts represent my and others' belief in my future earning ability.

I live in an abundant world.

I accept prosperity and abundance into my life.

I have a unique contribution to make.

I have a wealth of valuable skills and talents.

I invite and allow good to come into my life.

I change the world around me by changing myself.

Money is a source of good for myself and others.

The difference is that these statements about money represent a way of looking at money here and now rather than in the future. They don't relate to a different person from me i.e. someone who is "responsible", "careful with money", "a high earner", and so on.

And, as you consider the last set of statements above, you can feel more relaxed and less constrained. Your financial reality has not changed, but you begin to get a glimpse of how you can behave towards money in a different way when you think about money differently.

People who live the life they love are not necessarily wealthy; nor are they destitute; but they always have a mature relationship with money.

So how can we develop this understanding about money? How can we learn strategies which give us greater freedom around money? It is possible. You simply need to look, again, at the four levels of learning, and see which level reflects your own thinking about money.

Level 1 Behaviour, and money

We all began in the same place. There was a time when you did not have any attitude towards money, until you began to learn from others what money can mean. Babies and young children do not have any ideas about money. Tribes in different cultures use various bartering systems to express value and worth.

Level One ("All things are possible") is an appropriate place for children, but not for adults, because it is a naïve, child-like view of money: toy money, pretend money, money you don't have.

Level Two is where you experience the gap between the money you possess, and the money you would like to have. It is also here that you pick up deep, far reaching ideas about money which colour your entire understanding for many, many years. Here are some:

"There's never enough money"

"Your father doesn't earn enough"

"We can't go to the cinema/have a nice Christmas/go on holiday because we haven't any money."

"Money is the root of all evil."

"We'll never be rich."

"We can't afford it."

"I don't know where the next penny is coming from."

"Money doesn't grow on trees."

"You can't go to college/university because we can't afford the tuition."

Level Two money behaviour is where we make mistakes: we "fall over" and get bruised, in financial terms. This is when we learn that banks do not lend money for free; that we are expected to act responsibly and pay bills on time; that when we get a pay rise we feel fantastic for 24 hours and then wonder why we didn't receive more.

It is at Level Two2 that we learn to "give up".

Here are some typical thoughts we have around Level Two:

"...I'll never have enough money."

"...I can't handle money."

"...I'm always in debt."

"...I can't save."

You can probably add a few of your own:

"I...

"I...

"I...

But you know that Level Two behaviour and thinking about money - like all behaviours - are learned. So, how can you learn how to move from Level Two to Level Three, where you can begin to live a life that you love which includes a relationship with money that is beginning to be empowering and enjoyable?

First, take a deep breath, and say quietly to yourself, "It CAN be done."

You may have said something similar before, you may have tried to sort out your finances before and felt defeated, but we're not talking about then and there. We're talking about today, we're talking about now.

So, take another deep breath and say quietly to yourself again, "It CAN be done."

Get used to saying that. Regard it is a personal, secret saying, expressly for you, which you will only say to yourself in connection with financial issues.

Take another breath, "It CAN be done."

Be gentle with yourself; relax; don't tense your shoulders and clench your hands; get used to saying quietly and confidently to yourself, "It CAN be done" WITHOUT KNOWING - RIGHT HOW - WHEN IT WILL HAPPEN.

This is paradoxical, isn't it? "I know it can be done, but I don't know how!" It sounds crazy, but, in fact, that is how you learn, and this is how you move from Level Two to Level Three.

You don't know when you will actually ride that bike as well as your best friend, or your cousin, or your elder brother. But you do know that you will because you are committed to riding that bike, and riding it without falling off, and riding it better than anyone else in the street does.

Next, you need to accept that the situation you find yourself in about money is not the disaster that you think it is. In fact, the present situation is absolutely perfect.

This is the single great lesson that your feelings about money can teach you, and why it is so important to experience the pain and frustration that you attach to money, and the put-downs you pile on yourself when you don't earn enough, get hassled for over-spending.

Only as you develop strategies for really seeing reality as it is, without labels and packaging, can you begin to live the life you love.

And in order to begin to see the reality, you need to know exactly what your financial situation is. In detail, without flinching, without breaking out into a cold sweat, and without excuses and blame.

Look again at the first two exercises in this chapter. Can you identify the difference between them? It is this: the statements in the first exercise are vague, while the statements in the second statements are extremely precise.

And that shift from vague drifting to precise awareness is essential to living life to the full. Why? Because you know what that life is. It isn't a woolly, imprecise, "I'll know it when I recognise it life". It is a life that you can design for yourself down to the last, concrete detail.

Don't be afraid to take a big step.
You can't cross a chasm in two
small jumps

David Lloyd George

The fact is, you probably know what you need to do to reach financial independence. Until now, however, you haven't taken practical steps to do so.

Here are some suggestions:

Change your lifestyle: downshift.

Work on a cash basis and cut up your credit cards.

Cancel store cards.

Start looking at ways you can earn more money: ask for a pay raise; look at the vacancies.

Cut down on alcohol or any other toxic substance.

Change is achieved through small steps, one day at a time, and taking small actions, but taking them consistently and courageously.

There will be setbacks and disappointments, but you can discover a freedom and confidence you never imagined that you possessed. This is when you enter Level Four living in relationship to money.

Level Four Living: the golden rule about mastering money

Handling money issues calmly, maturely and professionally, will happen because you have discovered the golden rule about mastering money:

Your present financial situation is perfect.

Now, you may gulp when you read this, but it is the starting point, and the endgame, of moving from scarcity thinking to attract abundance into your life.

Your thinking and fantasising about money may be thrown into confusion by the Golden Rule, but when you begin living by it, you can immediately experience freedom from the financial issues which press down upon you.

You may not have all the money that you think you need, but you never will. You may not have the money or credit to buy what you want, but how many of your purchases that seemed to vital turned out to be so? You may not have the quality you would prefer, but that does not mean that you never will enjoy a different colour of prosperity.

When you start from the position that your financial situation is perfect, you gradually stop complaining, moaning and bitching about how dreadful things are, how unfair life is, and how wretched your money woes are. At a stroke, a whole raft of upsetting emotions can be cut loose and sent cascading over the waterfall.

What is left is the reality of the situation: that I have X amount of money. No more, no less. That is not good, bad, something to be ashamed of, something to blame someone else about, something to be angry and uptight or sleepless over.

When you start from the position that your financial situation is perfect, you no longer linger in the alleyways of the past "when things were better", nor will you dwell in an imaginary, wholly unreal future "when everything will be different".

Instead, you gradually learn to live in the present, the reality of the here and now. It is an immensely creative and powerful place to be, because you will find that you can say calmly, "I can" or "I can't" about money choices without feeling hard done by, or jealous of others.

You will have an adult, mature relationship with your finances that will be the envy of many, many people.

Question: I'm a single parent and really struggling. I feel sick every morning when I collect the post and see another letter from the bank or loan company. How can I begin to think that my present financial situation is perfect?

Answer: I really understand. Believe me, I've been there. And what I learned is this: that whether I thought it or not, and whether I think it's not - my life is perfect today. And so is yours. But don't rely on your feelings about it. Things are happening today that cause you pain. But that is not to say that it is going to go on for ever and always. I had to learn not to keep resisting what was going on in my life. Once I gradually learned to stop resisting, and to begin accepting, my financial situation began to change. So when I say that present is perfect, I am not saying that circumstances are what we would like them to be. It means that by accepting today - and all that it brings - is where we start from.

151

Fourteenth afternoon

For Those in Their 40s and 50s

This is often a time of deep involvement in career. It can also be a time when hopes are not fulfilled. Questions emerge that can help, or appear to threaten us: who are you? How far have you gone from your natural self? What do you have to do to get back to your normal self?

This is a tricky time! If you are in a career, you can begin to see how events are shaping. Maybe everything is going fine, but it is possible that goals which seemed attainable a few years back, now appear more distant than ever.

And this applies to relationships as well - surely, you ask, it can't be that difficult to enjoy a relationship with someone special. Equally, is it an impossible dream to find that special person?

And, of course, maybe everything is fine - and that is the issue. Everything is just too comfortable! And you realise that if you are going to make a change, it is going to have to be now.

Carl Jung wrote that life began at forty, or fifty, because up until then you are just doing research. In other words, it is this period of our lives when you find out what you really know, what you can really do, and - hopefully - what your destiny is.

You learn in this period of your life how to distinguish between knowledge and wisdom, between doing and being, and between our destination and destiny.

Knowledge and wisdom are the key distinctions at this period. It is likely that "knowing" how to achieve results is what has got you to where you are in life now. Knowing how to raise children, or run a department, or teach a class, or build a successful business. Knowledge is Level Two behaviour, which we refine and develop so that we are, often, increasing our capacity for learning.

Wisdom, however, is different. A wise person has learned how to channel their knowledge.

Before this period in your life, you may have focused on "doing" - the right University degree, a good job, the partner you love, living where you want. Now, however, you have the chance to focus on who you want to "be". There is no point devoting all your energies to climbing the ladder of success to find that you have leaned it against the wrong wall.

The world is full of people that have stopped listening to themselves or have listened only to their neighbours to learn what they ought to, how they ought to behave, and what the values are that they should be living for

Joseph Campbell

When we are concentrating on job, home, partners, or financial security, every milestone becomes a destination. We measure our success by these stopping points - vacations, Christmases, pay rises, bonus cheques, and birthdays - they appear on the mountain horizons, apparently a distant destination, which we then pass, and then find another one ahead.

In these years, however, you can learn to focus less on illusory destinations, and reflect on your destiny. How do I want to be remembered? What do I really want to enjoy about my life? Who really matters? What direction do I really want to be travelling? Because you do have time, still, to begin living a life that exceeds your expectations. You do not have to be ruled by what has gone before, by other's expectations or demands.

Now is the time to consider renewing friendships, and deepening those you already have. Friendships do need to be kept in good repair, and many people find that developing a successful career and raising a family combine to exclude all but the closest relatives.

At this period of your life, it may well be that you want to look again at perennial values: those issues of your heart, and spirit. You may well feel you have outgrown the beliefs or outlook that you grew up with, and experience a growing interest in inquiring further. Bring the same energy and common sense to this that you do in other areas of your life. Do not be surprised if you experience a resistance to this activity: you are re-engineering your fundamental personal outlook, which is never easy.

Here are ten questions to help your thinking:

1. What is worth making an effort for?

2. Is there a gap between what you believe, and what you really believe?

3. What is the greatest obstruction in your life at the moment?

4. What do you spend a lit of time worrying about?

5. What really is the priority in your life at the moment?

6. What touches you deeply?

7. What are your resources for change?

8. Is everything taking second place to money and career?

9. If you abandoned your interest in success, what would be different?

10. Ask yourself, "What do I want? Is it worthwhile?"

The focus of these questions is that they help us to develop a responsibility about our lives. At this period, it is all likely that our parents will require a greater response from ourselves in terms of care. Or, if you have grown apart, you will need to think through how you are going to feel when they are no longer around.

Equally, our children and dependants will themselves be developing their own lives. The major diversions for many adults - career and family - recede, and this time is when you have space and freedom to make choices for yourself.

You need to trust your intuition and personal hunches. You do know, inwardly, what you need to do, and who you need to be, to get back to your normal self.

It may require a series of demanding conversations with your partner, your company, or your family. It will almost certainly take longer than you expect. But you now have almost all of your resources in place to regain momentum and direction.

One key theme that many people find of increasing interest at this time is deepening their inner growth and investigating complementary insights into living - in other words, a deeper spirituality.

This will not necessarily be the belief system into which you were born, although it is quite likely that you can remain in this particular river of understanding, understanding in a more mature, adult way, its perennial wisdom. Many people, however, fell impelled to explore different traditions. You can bring the same commitment and care that you would to every endeavour, and still remain true to your natural self, and the life you love.

Perhaps the easiest way to let this period of your life unfold with vitality and energy is to develop a lightness of being. Don't allow the trappings of your job, a preoccupation with externals, the treadmill of status, or an unquenchable thirst for financial security, to deaden your spirit. It is too easy to become serious, solemn, unfunny and worthy. Allow others to follow that path if they wish - you will be so much more for yourself and others.

157

Fifteenth afternoon

Passion

We can rediscover the power of passion in our lives.

We can learn to be more open-minded and express ourselves more fully.

We can enjoy a greater openness and freedom in our life.

We can begin stepping forward with confidence, doing what we really love.

159

Living the life you love has a great deal - in fact, almost everything - to do with doing what you love.

If you love software design, then you will be a success in the information technology world. If your skill and enthusiasm is for clay pottery, then the potter's wheel is for you. If children give you your heart's satisfaction, then parenting or childcare will be your life's path. If you have always delighted in taking things apart and then re-assembling them, engineering will be your legacy.

It is not surprising to see that people who love what they do, love their life. They do not see any division between their work and their relaxation. Their vocation really is their vacation.

But many of us stifle what we love doing. We plod on from day to day, complaining about our work, and how awful it is, and how much we hate it, and how we wish we could do something else.

Only one thing stops us from doing what we love to do and living the life that we love. What is it? We don't do what we love doing because we are afraid of what the consequences might be.

For example, I don't go to evening classes to learn word processing because I'm afraid that I won't be able to finish the course.

I don't give up my day job because I am terrified of not having any money.

I don't tell my parents/partner/family that I love them because I am afraid of being ridiculed.

I don't tell my parents/family/friends about my sexuality because I am afraid of their rejection.

I don't tell my bank manager that his level of service is dire because I am afraid of losing my credit worthiness.

And so on.

The purpose of life is a life
of purpose

Robert Byrne

What it boils down to is this: you don't take some specific actions because you are afraid of the consequences.

We are extremely inconsistent about this. We live most of our life as though our acts have no consequences: in an extreme situation, for example, babies are often conceived because two people forget that making love might well have a specific consequence. More day-to-day examples might include "white" lying; petty theft from our place of work; overtaking when driving towards a blind corner; smoking; banned substance abuse; not making a will.

So on the one hand we live our lives as though there is no cause and effect; and then there are whole swathes of our lives that are wholly dominated by possible consequences which terrify us.

Notice the further inconsistency: it's odd, isn't it, that the consequences that we can be most certain of, say, the proven link between smoking and lung cancer, or alcohol abuse and dangerous driving, are often those that we treat most lightly. Consequences that might be far less reliably ascertained - destitution if we lose my job; ridicule if we change career - completely dominate our lives.

It is almost impossible to live the life you love when you are dominated by fears, "what ifs", or "in cases".

What you need to do is to redress the imbalance in your life between reality and fantasy. This will straighten out the distortion.

You experience a massive advance in your thinking in this area when you focus less on consequences, and more on meaning. Because consequences are "out there" and meaning is here and now. The difference between the consequence of something you do, and the meaning it has for you, is the difference between doing something because you have to, and living every moment of every day because of who you are.

When you live every moment of every day because of who you are, you will have discovered passion in your life, you will live passionately, and you will bring energy and enthusiasm to what we do.

This is the effect that passion has. It is like having your own personal oil well delivering crude energy to your life that you can process and refine in any way you choose.

Passion is like the fastest processing chip in your own life computer.

Passion for living allows you to live an incredible life, achieve your desires and handle each and every obstacle in a way that is absolutely unique to you.

When you live a life a life of passion, you focus on what matters to you, not what is dictated by someone else.

When you live a life of passion, you integrate meaning and value in your life, rather than pay lip service to an impersonal code of ethics unthinkingly.

When you a life of passion, you are able to see how everything fits together, in its place and part in your jigsaw lives, rather than be dwarfed and overwhelmed by circumstances.

> *A ship in harbour is safe, but that's*
> *not why ships are built*
>
> John Shedd

Research has shown that people who have passion in their lives have healthier bodies, sleep better and are more relaxed.

So how do we discover the passion of our life?

Here is some background information.

First, discovering your passion does not necessarily happen in a blinding flash of light, but it is more than possible that you actually do know, deep down, what it is. Really - you do, but even to whisper it to yourself might seem so outlandish and impractical that it is better to keep it locked up in that attic room of your heart with other dreams and hopes that you have given up on.

163

Next, discovering your passion is rather like finding that the strongest rope is made up of different strands. So you can use several skills and enthusiasms to uncover your passion, rather than think that you have to find something unique.

Then, you need to relax and gently laugh at yourself. After all, you may have spent 10, 20 or more years hiding your passion under layers of other activities: career, financial security, relationships, the quest for enlightenment, and to imagine that you can just uncover your passion after a moment's reflection is unrealistic.

It could be so, if every day for the last 10 years you have laboured in a job you hated and spent every spare moment mapping the precise route you will take to climb to the top of Mount Everest to achieve your secret desire. In this instance, you know what your passion in life is - climbing - but you have stifled it.

So it may be that your passion is staring you in the face; more likely, though, it needs to be untangled and unravelled to be seen clearly.

Here are some ideas for doing this:

Go for a lazy walk. It could be in the park; it might be in the country; perhaps it is by the river or a lake: water is tremendously calming and freeing up. This walking exercise is best done on its own, so don't combine it with carrying the shopping back to the apartment, or walking to the Tube station.

Take time to dawdle, wander, look at the intricate pattern of bark on trees, or follow a bird's flight along the path, through the trees and under a bridge. Enjoy the sparkle of sun on wet grass, or the shapes that clouds make in the sky.

What you are doing in this walk is allowing your mind space. More accurately, you are giving yourself room to think the unthinkable...what if? What would it take? What might it be?

Maybe 50 different ideas come and go; maybe 100; but more likely it will be one or two or three core ideas that you have had for a long time.

Don't make any decisions about these ideas or plans or goals; don't make any choices; just start getting used to taking them seriously, and not pushing them away. Because for as long as you have been resisting them, you have been resisting what is most attractive, desirable, engaging and terrific about yourself!

There are two ways to live your life. One is as though nothing is a miracle. The other is as though everything is a miracle

Albert Einstein

Here is an exercise you can do right now if you go for a walk and nothing seems to be present.

Take a pen and complete the following sentence:

"If I won the lottery today and could do whatever I wanted, I would....."

Just notice if there is any resistance even to writing these plans. You see, we spend so much time at Level Two where we learn to give up, putting plans on one side "..until the time is right" that it seems to be absolutely natural.

But because we are such good learners, and because we have taken so many years to perfect this skill, it is hard to accept that there is a stepping stone beyond the one we are standing on.

165

So don't get angry with yourself, or inwardly put yourself down, or succumb to some kind of "Why can't I get it together?" routine. The good news is that you've probably played these inner tape cassettes so long that they are almost worn out. Don't throw them out - just let them be.

Here is another exercise, which will allow you to discover your life's passion.

Find a time when you are relaxed and not in a mad hurry. Play your favourite CD of soothing, calming music. Settle down, and allow your mind to wander. Think back to a time when you were incredibly happy. Recall special memories. Allow yourself to enjoy them.

Among those memories will be recollections of an activity where you were really successful. It may have been when you were a child, painting a smudged picture which was pinned on the wall, or as a student when you organised the graduation party. Perhaps it was as a junior manager when you handled a crisis superbly.

Or, maybe it was the way you took care of your best friend when she was hospitalised.

Allow your memory freedom, and enjoy the memories. They are there for a reason, and these recollections have a purpose. There is something in you that wants you to remember.

There will be one memory, or a cluster of memories, that give you special pleasure. This will be a signpost to your passion. Don't jump to a conclusion, but ask your memory what it wants to say to you. And ask gently! Don't demand.

Don't be surprised if nothing seems to happen. You have spent a long time learning not to listen to your inner wisdom, so it would be strange if you suddenly heard clearly. Trust your powers of self-awareness.

The truth is, your passion will find you. That is why some descriptions of passion have been likened to a voice calling us. In fact, some passions which are easily identified, such as a passion for helping others in healthcare (medicine and nursing) or ministering to others within a religious tradition (the priesthood or rabbinical training) or working to resolve conflicts (the legal profession) are traditionally called "vocations", or "callings."

A vocation is a calling, and there are famous stories of women and men whose sense of vocation was so powerful that it allowed them to achieve tremendous goals.

Make your life a mission - not
an intermission

Arnold Glasgow

Discovering your passion in life involves learning to listen to yourself. You have to learn to hear what is going on within. This takes skill, and it's a great skill to learn. Sometimes it is called intuition, which is a powerful ability to grasp something without necessarily having all the information. Sometimes the words "self knowledge" sum up the ability to listen to your heart's desire.

What follows next is that you learn to live with your passion, and allow it to infuse and shape your life.

Think of a teabag. Pour hot water over the teabag, and the whorls and spirals of the tea infuse the water until the drink is ready. That is what it is like as you discover your passion.

167

Being passionate in life need not mean that your passion takes over your life. For example, a high-flying financial services executive is passionately committed to her role as a mother. A high school teacher is a passionate mountaineer. An American publisher takes tai chi classes with a world respected teacher in Asia three times a year. A nurse goes freefall parachuting every weekend.

These are instances where individuals have integrated their passion into their lives. They don't lead lives of frustration, neither doing what they love, nor complaining inwardly to themselves and others.

A component of a passionate life is that others know what your passion is. They will be aware of its meaning for you, and its value for you. Being part of a group that is supportive of your passion also provides a certain realism: off piste skiing, for instance, is a natural interest of a passionate skier, but skiing friends can also bring healthy caution if the conditions are dangerous. It is the same with scuba diving, or weightlifting.

Questions to ask about my passion:

Is it something I can share with others?

Does it involve danger to myself, or to others?

Is it legal?

Is it ethical?

It is your passion that gives value to your life, and direction too.

So many people find that their day is dominated by wanting something. This can become an overwhelming motivator that just has to be satisfied immediately. You see a sugary cake, and want it now. You go past a bar and want a drink now. You see a pretty woman/attractive man and have to flirt now, even if one part of you does not really want to. It is as if you have no energy at all to resist. You have no "choice energy". Your reservoir is empty.

However, when your passion is aligned with the rest of your life, a subtle change takes place which gives us tremendous freedom and choice energy. This is because your passion gives you meaning, and gives energy to your values.

What's more important - your goal?
Or others' opinions of your goal?

Peter McWilliams

So that cream cake scenario could take a different turn: "I'm passionate about healthy eating, so even though it looks delicious, I'll pass". Or, "I'd love this latest computer software, but I'm passionate about financial freedom, so I will buy it when I can afford it." Or, "She (or he) is really good looking, and I'm attracted to her (or him) but I'm passionate about integrity, so I won't go back to her/his place."

Obviously, the danger in individual examples is that they can seem prissy, but nonetheless, you can see the different energy available.

A life of passion means that you have freedom and energy to choose.

169

People who lead lives that they love have freedom. You can have it too.

———————

Question: Can you explain more about doing something because of who I am, rather than because I have to, and how that links with passion?

Answer: If you are passionate about life you are fully engaged in everything that you do. You're interested, you're excited, and you're absorbed. Now, the activity or task may be extremely mundane, even dull, but rather than squeeze meaning from it - "This is awful" - you can bring meaning to it: "I am someone who enjoys learning how to live fully from moment to moment." As you learn to do this more skilfully, you will find that you can bring a passion and zest for living to any activity, not because you have to, but because that's how you are.

Question: Can my passion change? Is it something that is the same for ever?

Answer: Of course your passions change, although sometimes people have a specific focus that remains throughout life. Most of us find that as we grow and develop, and our circumstances evolve, so our passions mature and shift also.

Summary

Many of us stifle what we love doing.

Passion restores our integrity and wholeness.

We can discover and re-discover our passion.

Trust that our passion will find us. Allow it to happen.

Sixteenth afternoon

Dieting Isn't Just About Food

Many of us use food/sex/money to cope with our upsets.

Most of us are probably well aware of the food choices we 'should' be making.

We get stuck in yo-yo situations.

We can learn to live lives with greater freedom in the areas of food, weight, self-image.

These issues are wholly legitimate, and part of growing emotionally and spiritually.

Just as most of us know what we "ought" to do when there's a problem, nearly all of us are aware of the food choices that we "should" be making. But we don't, and the result is that we become miserable, filled with disappointment and worthlessness. "Heavens - if I can't even resist that last half slice, it just shows how useless I am."

Sometimes, this ability to master our ability to choose becomes a destructive and an overriding objective. "Look how good I am - I have resisted eating/drinking for 8/10/12 hours. Aren't I strong?" All too soon, we're overwhelmed with shame when we fall short of our self-imposed standards that are impossible to maintain.

Often the way people feel about food, and their bodies, is the way they feel about many other things as well. Some have similarly self-critical feelings about their sexuality, about their sexual needs, about their alcohol addiction (or near-addiction), the hours they spend watching television or the money they spend shopping, buying golf accessories, clothes or computer software that they simply do not want. But, for fleeting moments, they feel better before they yo-yo back to blaming themselves and criticising themselves for not being "better" or "stronger".

This is why dieting isn't just about food. It's about "success" and "failure", but living life in such a stark black and white manner is wholly ineffective.

The trouble is, most of us adopt the same ineffective approach to other areas of our lives as well. In every case, we usually only succeed in intensifying our preoccupation with food and weight, and lowering our self-esteem. Other people may not focus excessively on weight related issues, but they substitute money, children, status or other thinly disguised obsessions.

As you learn to live the life you love, however, you can learn to safely and gently disentangle the complicated web that you have woven around simple words like "food", "weight", or "money" and "sex" and "family".

The way we live our days is the way we live our lives

Annie Dillard

Level One learning and dieting

We need, first, to begin at the beginning, and without any self-judgment, calmly start looking back through your mental scrapbook for clues about the way you learned about food, and weight, and how you looked.

This need not be a deeply introspective exercise; in fact, it's better to be light hearted and relaxed.

Remember, Level One learning is when we realised that we couldn't do something, or wanted to do something, or be someone and decided to do something about it. Maybe we were laughed at; maybe the dress size wasn't what we thought it ought to have been, and so on.

Level Two learning and dieting

At Level Two we chose to adopt certain practices that we believed would change things. Maybe it was a diet; maybe it was focusing on weight; perhaps it was joining a support group. Whatever it was, it did not produce the results we wanted and - we gave up!

"Giving up" is the Level Two experience. Yo-yo dieting is simply going round and round from Level One (deciding to do something) to Level Two (giving up). The depression and misery experienced by so many good, clever, wise, loving, intelligent, wonderful people is because they come to believe that there is no way out of this vicious circle. This sense of failure dominates their lives, and the idea of living a life that they love becomes like a desert mirage.

Level Three and dieting

Level Three dieting occurs when we suddenly experience a core transformation: I can do it. And this comes about, remember, because we have remembered our successful learning situations:

Successful learning for effective relationship with food, and every other life spoiling preoccupation:

> Find support. If you are having a tough time with food, it is a stark fact that you are not alone, and that there are many others who share your problem. Find a group (or start one) where you can learn to reduce your anxiety, hear new ideas, rather than endlessly recycling those old, unhelpful self-critical tapes in your head.

> Find information. If you are struggling with the dieting yo-yo, be relentless in acquiring the correct knowledge and skills you need. The most powerful learning breakthrough will come when you suddenly distinguish between what is known about dieting, and what is commonly believed to be the truth.

Level Four learning and dieting

This is when it comes together. And it will be OK. When you enjoy Level Four in this area of living, you won't be focusing on food, but could be hugely more aware of your health. You won't be worrying about your physical size, but able to love and enjoy your body; and really will be friends with the person you see in the mirror. Rather than worrying about not having friends or

We all get the God we believe in

Julia McCarthy

what people think about you, you could be contributing to, and part of, a support group who empower you to challenge size-bigotry and fight discrimination wherever you find it.

Other life preoccupations

Sex: "I don't get enough/I don't love enough/I'm ashamed of it."

Money: "I don't have enough/I'll never be rich/bankruptcy is a hideous failure."

Career: "I can't even conceive of changing my job and my work is (actually) more important to me than anyone or anything."

Speaking in public: "I would die rather than give a speech; I couldn't ever complain about shoddy service/goods."

In every case, you can learn to move on from where you have given up, and move to a level of experience which is quite different. And you do so by remembering that you learned how to think about ourselves in the way that preoccupies your every thought, you learned how to feel depressed about ourselves, and you learned how to measure your life by how much you eat/spend/make love.

You can also learn how to be at peace with yourself. The whole dieting issue for many women has been trivialised and treated with enormous insensitivity, just as every other variation from the "norm" is considered a sign of "weakness" or "failure".

By learning to like yourself, and take care of yourself, whether it be in the area of diet, money, or relationships, you can become yourself a role model of freedom for others who may be suffering in silence.

Q uestion: Are you saying that if I focus on everything except food, I will lose weight?

A nswer: No. What I'm asking is this: how important is this weight loss in your life? And that question has to be asked within the context of larger questions. These questions could be: does your genetic history get in the way of your fascination with being thin? How does severe dieting affect you physically and emotionally? To what degree does an obsession with food get in the way of your leading a normal life? It may be really important to get rid of the weighing scales; chuck them out. Get greater, validated information about dieting. Learn how to increase your self-esteem, and learn as much as possible about healthier lifestyle choices and improved eating patterns.

Q uestion: I'd like to know more about other preoccupations, such as status, and how they relate to dieting?

A nswer: The dynamics underlying dieting issues are not dissimilar to other life-denying preoccupations such as serial shopping, workaholism, or even social lying. At their deepest core, all these profound upsets are related to how you see yourself, or rather, how you don't want to see yourself. Once you are at peace with the reality of your greatness as a human being, other freedoms will begin to flow. But it is not just a matter of thinking about it and expecting - click - for your life to change magically. In real time, with the support of warm, understanding and like-minded friends, you will find that profound change in these areas of your life will occur.

Q uestion: What do you mean when you say that I won't know, at the beginning, how it will be when I am more relaxed about dieting?

Answer: Simply, there is a danger that you can unwittingly put limits on what is possible for you. If you are in a yo-yo dieting situation, or in financial straits, or find that the only way to find release from upset at work is to go shopping, it might be that the only change you can envisage is a yo-yo reaction: a faultless body, untold riches, or never working again. These extremes - which are perfectly understandable - are only one set of outcomes, however. As you learn to live a life you love in the area of food, your body, money or work, you find that you become more open to other possibilities.

179

Summary

We all need to learn to understand how our relationship with food (or money etc) has developed in our lives.

We can all move on from the yo-yo situations we find ourselves in.

We can all get information and the support of others who are interested in not emphasising weight loss as the only measure of good health. We can insist in size-blind, size-informed health guidance. We can learn to appreciate the diversity of human sizes and shapes and recognise the beauty, strength and grace in all of them.

We can enjoy, anticipate and explore the many possibilities that lie ahead of us as we grow stronger and more confident around about our size and weight.

Seventeenth evening

Facing Our Fear - Bereavement and Death

> The untimely death of a relative, a child, or a partner is shattering. Everything we take for granted, especially our own sense of immortality - that we will live until a ripe old age - is broken. It can seem impossible for us to live fully after a bereavement or if we are faced with a life threatening illness. But, we can learn profound lessons about living as we learn to manage our fears about death. It is not gloomy to do so. It is deeply mature, because we are learning to understand what our lives are really about.

How can it happen? Why does it happen? Why me? Why them? Why?

We've all asked ourselves those questions. We'll go on doing so. And often, with a timing that seems cruel, these questions raise themselves like stinging nettles or poison ivy in a beautiful garden, just when we least expect them.

Babies die prematurely after their parents have longed to conceive, and the mother has carried her child with more love than she dare breathe; young adults die in horrific accidents; best friends suffer painful, drawn out deaths; our parents lose their senses, and all understanding of their being. We walk into the consultant's office and know the worst before she even speaks to us.

Why?

Most of the time we are anaesthetised to death and suffering because they happen out there to other people, not to our own friends' babies, not our own best friends, not even to ourselves, until the unexpected happens.

When we put the telephone down after someone has given us shocking news, it is not unusual to feel hypocritical, false, and deceitful: "How can I live a life that I love when other people are suffering so much?"

At a deeper level, we ask ourselves, how can I live a life that I love when I am really, really frightened?

Let's look at causes of fear which have been identified in people with life threatening illness:

Fear of separation from loved people, homes, jobs.

Fear of becoming a burden to others.

The aim of life is to be fully born,
though it's a tragedy is that most
of us die before we are thus born

Eric Fromm

Fear of losing control.

Fear for dependants.

Fear of pain.

Fear of being unable to complete our responsibilities
or tasks that really matter to us.

Fear of dying

Fear of being dead

Fear of the fears of others about our imminent death.

There's one fact we can be certain of: we are all going to die, and
our hopes and dreams are all affected by that stark reality. Being
afraid of death is not a sign of weakness; it is an integral part of
our survival instinct that protects and guides us from dangerous
situations. Quite often, with the advent of sophisticated
treatment of pain and the growth of hospice centres for
terminally ill patients, it is no longer the fear of pain that worries
us, but what to do about our fears.

Fear can paralyse us. We can wake in the middle of the night in
the inky darkness and feel terribly lonely, vulnerable and afraid.
We can grieve for all that is not to be, and alternate wildly
between hope and despair.

But human beings are pretty tough.

It is possible - still being gentle on yourself, to find sense and
meaning, peace and serenity, calm and power - to deal with
whatever life brings you.

First, if you feel it is the right time for you to do so, gently
confront the scary situation over and over again. Accurate and

reliable information from informed professionals reduces anxiety and worry; finding others who may be walking the same path as you, and talking to one of them with whom you feel an affinity helps enormously to get some perspective. Maybe there is support that can be got from a self-help group, or a special friend.

You could also try keeping a journal. Don't think of it as a diary; simply commit to letting your hand write across three sides of paper. Don't attempt to write great prose or fancy phrases, just write whatever your hand lets you.

It might be that you write "I'm angry" "I'm angry" "I'm angry" or "Why me?" "Why me?" for three pages. So what? You will feel differently afterwards because you have been able to express honestly the frustration you are feeling. The more you can get those strong emotions off your chest, the more you will learn to counter your fears directly.

Then, channel your "fear energy" into positive activities. Write a card to someone you have been out of touch with; telephone a friend; tidy that cupboard you have been meaning to clean out but never got round to doing.

If you believe that feeling bad or worrying long enough will change a fact, then you are residing on a different planet with a different reality system

Wayne Dyer

At times of great stress and fear, even if you may feel physically or spiritually bereft, your life can be of enormous value for others. Simply by being the people you are, even if you feel you are pushing your wheelbarrow uphill and against the wind, others will gain strength and comfort from you.

If you are faced with the wholly unexpected and painful, you can learn to challenge your irrational beliefs and demands of how things "should" be.

Above all, you can learn to live fully in the present moment, and really value every day that is given to you. As you do so, you are able to face problems squarely, and learn to take action.

Coping with bereavement and death is not easy. But it becomes easier if we are a little prepared by at least giving some thought now, rather than later, to our own mortality, and purpose in life.

If we knew that our world, as we know it, would cease to be in six hours, we would probably only say three words to everyone who is close to us, even strangers. These words would be, "I love you".

This is why suffering the pain of bereavement can be seen as one of life's toughest privileges, because someone else who died has given us the gift of seeing the value of our own life.

Facing the reality of our own being - the fact that we grow, live, and die - is probably the most powerful journey we can make to understand how to live our life fully.

Illness, pain suffering and bereavement are great teachers. They can help us to learn the depth of what it means to live lives that we love.

Empty your mind of all thoughts.
Let your heart be at peace.
Each separate being in the universe
returns to the common source.
You can deal with whatever life brings you,
and when death comes, you are ready.

Lao-tzu, The Book of the Way, trans. Stephen Mitchell

186

Question: How does learning to confront my own fears about death help others?

Answer: One of the greatest gifts you can give anyone is to understand them without judging. To be compassionate means to share someone's pain or suffering. When you learn to understand your own fear of death, you can really share another's fear. You don't have to use fancy words or counselling jargon. You only need to say truthfully - "I understand" - for the other person to completely get that you do.

Question: Isn't there a danger of becoming cold and clinical by focusing on death?

Three things in human life are important. The first is to be kind. The second is to be kind. And the third is to be kind

Henry James

A nswer: Not at all. In fact, completely the opposite occurs. Inexperienced health professionals often deny their own fears of death, and feelings of failure, by trying to become "clinical" in the face of a patient dying. Wiser practitioners realise what is happening, and discover their own ability to provide a deeper healing occurs as they admit their own anxieties about death.

Q uestion: Isn't all this talk about death a bit depressing?

A nswer: If it's all that is talked about, yes! But it's even more depressing if it's never even thought about!

Summary

It's easy to be frightened about death and dying.

We can learn to manage our fear of death, and in doing so, other fears too.

The way we do so affects other areas of our life for the better.

We can learn profound lessons from those who are ill, or suffer, or are dying.

We will only - truly - lead lives that we love when we are wholly at peace with the prospect of our own death.

Eighteenth evening

Success, Work and Career

> We make success hard for ourselves. But we can learn to discover how successful we are in reality, and how great our potential for success is.
>
> Success is based on understanding our values, not on meeting our needs.

Most of us succeed in spite of ourselves. That is to say, by and large we achieve enough to get by, sometimes better than we hope, normally enough to survive from day to day without too much hassle and setback. But we succeed in spite of ourselves because sometimes we sabotage our best intentions.

The vital job application gets posted late. Or the important immigration form is not filled in accurately, or we fluff a job interview by arriving late, jittery, and do not perform as well as we know we would have done if we had only taken a few more minutes to check that we knew the location of the company we had to visit.

But is that a fair description of living a life that we love? Hardly!

We have learned to put up with a level of living that is tolerable, but not so wonderful that we can honestly say that every day is exactly perfect.

More than anything else, we allow what we do for a living to define what we imagine other people believe about us. After all, almost the first thing someone asks another after a few moments small talk is "What do you do?".

If we have a job, we spend more time with our colleagues than we do with our partner; in fact, many people feel more relaxed at work than they do in their own homes. Research shows that we are nicer to people at work, and show them greater respect and tolerance, than we do to those in our non-work environments.

But our work environment often presents the greatest challenge to living the life we love. In fact, the office environment becomes a microcosm of life itself!

How you feel about work is often a good test about how you feel about your life, and how you live it.

If your tolerate less pay than you believe you deserve, do nothing about it but moan to your partner, it might indicate how you behave in other areas of your life. If you consistently take advantage of colleagues, taking credit where it isn't due, undermining other people's efforts etc, it is a sure bet that you are like that in other areas of your life as well.

The road to success is always
under construction

Lilly Tomlin

And, of course, you can see the opposite situation at work as well. We all know the person who we can ask to help when we have to meet a deadline; who to turn to when something really needs to be turned around in a hurry; who to trust with a confidence and know that it will not get repeated.

So you can be grateful for your work situation because it is a mini laboratory to begin to understand how to live the life you love. At work, it is easy to look on the surface of your life and see what is missing. It might be money, it might be the actual job itself, it could be the people you work with, it might be the hours: the details are like brushstrokes which complete the picture of your life.

And, as in so many other areas of living, there is part of us which says, "That's the way it is. It is not going to change. I have to put up with it".

This is a good point to pause, remember the four levels of learning, and recall that if you feel like this, you are stuck at Level Two, and showing how well you learned "how to give up!".

Exercise:

Many work environments are unhealthy, psychologically and physically. No one benefits from weak leadership, or frequent changes of strategy; everybody suffers when there are unrealistic project milestones producing chronic overwork. All too often, companies tread just one inch the wrong side of legality when it comes to economic exploitation through inadequate pay and overwork. In spite of emails and company Intranets there can be poor communication between different parts of the organisation. Often there is unfair evaluation and favouritism: acknowledgement is rarely given for a job well done. There can be lack of compassion for people who are hurting outside their workplace.

Above all, there are three invisible flags which fly outside every corporate building, government agency, academic institution, engineering plant and retail unit. Each flag has one word embroidered on it. The first flag carries the word "Apathy", the second, "Resignation" and the third, "Cynicism".

Apathy, Resignation and Cynicism are the enemies of business life and they affect each and every one of us. If we are to live lives that we love, not just at weekends, in the evenings and when we're on holiday, we have to learn how to beat them. Until we do, we will not be living life to the full.

We all know the cynic, the person who has given up but not shut up. Someone who is resigned has given up and shut up. And the person who has given in to apathy has given up, shut up, and is deeply fed up!

So, there are inward and outward aspects to our work. The outward aspects, money, acknowledgement, and career development, require one set of strategies. But to really live the life you live, you need to look at the inward aspects as well: apathy, resignation and cynicism.

The fact is, we have all learned how to be cynical at work. Cynicism raises a laugh, but it is as corrosive and destructive as

For true success ask yourself these four questions: Why? Why not? Why not me? Why not now?

Jimmy Dean

acid. Many people are deeply cynical about living a life that can be loved, and they resent anyone who begins to explore what that possibility could mean.

Resignation is like glue, or heavy industrial oil that is long past its usefulness. Resignation slows down the machinery of business life because "we tried that before and it didn't work..." and "there's no point doing that because..." and "we don't do things like that around here...".

Apathy is a Level Two living where there is a complete lack of passion and involvement in life. The attitude is, "they just don't care - so what? So long as I get my pay check, I will do the minimum".

If you are to live the life you love, you need to sort out your complex, love-hate feelings about work. And this requires a sense of humour, balance and common sense. Few of us can just walk into the boss's office and say, "I'm off. I've decided to live the life I love and a key component of that is never seeing you again. Goodbye!"

And it is not unusual for you to look back at any part of your life and recognise that things could have been different. You might have taken that job, or written that article, or remained with that boy/girlfriend/spouse.

And other people often appear more successful than you do! Other people, it seems, do not make the mistakes you do; earn more than you do; look better than you do; don't have arguments and rows the way you do; even, seem to behave better than you do.

Is this true? Probably not! But the way you look at your own "success" and the way you think of other people's "success" is very revealing.

On one hand, the self-portrait you have of your own apparent lack of success in life resembles one of those paint-by-number craft pictures, except that are only two colours, Success and Failure, and the Success paint tub is empty, while there is lots of Failure paint to use up.

We are much more tolerant of other people than we are of ourselves, and one of the key lessons in living the life that we love is learning to become more tolerant and accepting of ourselves, and, to begin acknowledging our own successes.

Exercise:

Rather than saying "I did this today..." Substitute "I am someone who.... In the present tense"

1. "I typed six reports, scheduled the department meetings and had to act as secretary to the Dean's meeting..."

becomes

> "I am someone who can juggle several tasks and still get things done.."

2. "Another typical day. I got the kids to school, tidied the apartment, sorted Frank's room and did the weekly shop.."

becomes

> "I am someone who values my family and is a skilful single parent."

3. "I met with personnel and reviewed Mark's record. We had a meeting after lunch and I explained that his absenteeism affected the entire project. He agreed with my assessment about his future with us."

becomes

"I am someone who is prepared to take action."

4. "I did............"

can become

"I am someone who............"

Whether you are successful or not is rather like the half-full and half-empty bottle. What counts for success for one person may well not count at all for in someone else's eyes.

A good example of this might be someone who earns a high income. His or her subordinates might think that she is extremely successful, because she earns lots of money. However, another person's spouse might have quite another view: he is never at home, never helps with the housework, never spends time with their children, and so on.

Another example of success might be a glamorous, world famous catwalk model. Recognisable on every magazine cover, and the centre of attention wherever she stays, it comes as a shock to discover that, in fact, she does not think she is a success at all. She never finished school; never went to university; has suffered a string of unhappy relationships which were brutally dissected by the tabloids in every continent and has an eating disorder. Yet millions of readers yearn for what she has.

Success is based on values. If your values are solely based on money, then the only scorecard you have to register your successes will be a financial one.

If your values are centred around relationships, or a particular relationship, then your gauge of success will depend on whether you are "in a relationship".

Your success is based on your values not someone else's. Learning to live the life you love is learning to make decisions about what really matters to you. Not what your partner/work colleagues/congregation/club/political association think. Of course, there may well be common ground but the starting point is establishing your values.

What is really important to you? What is your ache in life? What really matters?

We can learn something from large organisations who spend millions working out if they are successful. And they do not simply rely on money indicators. A successful business will be judged on how its employees are treated, whether their staff turnover is higher than their competitors', for instance. Nowadays, any large multinational is assessed on its ethical stance - does it employ cheap or illegal labour overseas to satisfy its home market? And how about its environmental policy?

So a company's success is not just assessed according to how much money it earned for shareholders. While that is still important, other factors come into play.

Many companies have tried to incorporate these success measurements into words, often called Mission Statements, that spell out for employees, customers and interested observers what the company considers key components of success.

Accept praise. But don't inhale

Basil Hume

In order to judge success, then, we need to have measurements.

Look at long distance truck drivers. Increasingly, if you drive behind one on the motorway, you will see a sticker asking you if the truck is being driven carefully. If not, there is a Freefone number to call if you wish to make a complaint. So, in this case, there is a measurement - road courtesy - to monitor the truck driver's "success".

So, what are your measures for success? What are the values that matter to you?

We each have five types of value:

1. Physiological values: the basic values connected with our physical lives.

2. Safety values: security and the absence of threat and fear. These values are often future orientated and include the need to ensure that the physiological needs will continue to be met in the near future.

3. Affiliation values: acceptance, belonging, support, affection, friendship and love.

4. Esteem values: self-esteem and the esteem of others. They include personal feelings of achievement and being perceived by others as successful. We value self-respect and the respect of others who matter to us.

5. Self-actualisation values: the vital components of personal growth as we move more and more towards living the live we love. These values manifest themselves in the ability to understand and grow through our limitations, and come close and closer to attaining our full potential.

These five sets of values interlink, because if you are hungry (not satisfying your physiological values) then you are less concerned with other people (affiliation values). If you are afraid of losing your job (safety values) you will put your self-actualisation values on the back burner.

In other words, the different values form a ladder of priorities.

Often, without realising it, you discover that the values that are active in your life are clustered on one rung of the value ladder. Teenagers, for example, are almost wholly concerned with affiliation values. They have to wear the right trainers and the current logo. People who grew up in poor neighbourhoods often live lives that are dominated by physiological values because their parents worried continually about where the next meal was coming from. On the other hand, many people come across as wholly self-absorbed, focusing on personal enlightenment, or the latest self-help therapy: their values are clustered almost exclusively around the fifth self-actualisation rung.

When you understand more clearly what your own values are, you can begin to live a life that is more closely aligned with them because they will be manifestly apparent in the way you live from day to day.

A mature measure of success is the degree to which you learn to live a life where the five value groups are represented approximately equally.

Expressions of physiological values

> Healthy lifestyle: e.g. better sleep; less alcohol/nicotine; more zest; regular exercise; stress reduction.

Expressions of safety values

> Money; career; personal environment.

Examples of affiliation values

Relationships: finding Mr/Mrs Right; friends; biological and wider family.

Examples of esteem values

Loving yourself; the ability to make requests and to say "no"; being at ease on your own and in a crowd.

Examples of self actualisation values

Spirituality: beginning a path of recovery; developing a personal life plan; making big life changes.

You can begin to live a life you love when you orient your life around these five areas of value. This can take time - you will need to be gentle and realistic - but it can be done!

Exercise:

1. For the next seven days, take one value area and take five steps to make it real in your life.

These steps need not be extravagant, but simple and easy to do. So for the Esteem value area:

Request detailed information in the supermarket about organic food.

Spend an enjoyable evening on your own.

Spend an entire day saying "no" graciously.

2. Design an exciting project to fully express one value area and make it real in your life.

Taking the Safety value area:

Redecorate your entire flat.

Completely re-organise your computer hard disc (but back-up before you do anything!).

Consciously pick up obvious litter and don't make a big deal about it.

3. Re-organise your life around the five value areas.

Adjust your priorities.

Change job.

Plan to move to where you really want to live.

It isn't easy to do all of this overnight. Remember that values have power in your life when you choose to manifest them in your life. They have greater effect when you tell someone who is close to us about your intention. However, the greatest transformation is available to you when you also express your intention to live a life aligned to value within the wider community of which you are a part, outwardly and publicly.

Q uestion: Can you tell me more about "succeeding in spite of yourself"?

A nswer: All of us are successful. It is no mean feat to be an adult! Often, however, without realising, you set limits on your success: you "plateau" and don't realise that there are still exciting vistas and prairies ahead. Also, you can make success hard work because you do not handle stuff that gets in the way. If you're rude, for instance, you may still get to the top of the tree, but there will be any number of people hoping it gets blown down. If you haven't learned to be responsible around money issues, you may earn a high income and appear to be very successful, and yet be massively in debt.

Question: I'm a single parent. I only just manage to get by. It sounds incredibly unrealistic to talk about changing jobs as though it can be done with a wave of a magic wand.

Answer: Changing jobs is never straightforward, especially when you are juggling myriad responsibilities. But when you allow space in your life to enjoy the different value areas rather than live in a state of permanent anxiety and frustration, changes begin to occur. You will do it, I promise.

Summary

Success is not about having things, but living by our values.

We can discover our core values.

We can learn to live lives that are centred around them.

Nineteenth evening

Deepening Our Love and Relationships

We are born to love and to be loved.

Amazing relationships are not the result of luck or chance.

We can re-learn how to enjoy relationships, and attract love into our life.

Forgiveness is the superhighway to true, lasting love.

We are born to love, and it is our destiny to be loved. That is a truth, and it is a truth that can set us free when we're upset, hurt and disappointed.

We are also born to love far more than we can dream we are capable. And it is our destiny to be loved more deeply than we can ever imagine.

On any given day, we are probably somewhere on a line between those two positions. One day we're living in the rainbow. Another, it seems that there is nothing but storm clouds and the heaviest rain.

But it doesn't always work out smoothly, does it? You can have the most perfect time with your partner, who you love more than anyone else on this planet, and suddenly find yourself in a horrible argument.

You can be married, or living in a committed way with somebody, and suddenly, crazily, realise that he or she isn't who you can spend the rest of your life with.

Your children can be the most important people in your life. Then you find yourself staring at the green traffic light, lost in thought until an angry driver behind you honks their horn, and realise that you may have to move out of your children's home, leave them and all you hold dear, because someone else has entered your life.

You can get dumped on too. Slaving away in a poorly paid job to support a partner through business school, and you're chucked for somebody else. Or, deciding not to follow your heart's desire to work in a low paid vocation, and be happy, but continue to work in a highly paid rat-race job, you find out that your partner has cheated on you for years and is now still suing you for financial support.

For the most part, you cross our fingers and hope that it won't happen to you. Or, that it will. For people who do not enjoy a

We can choose to make our love
for each other what our lives are
really about

Werner Erhard

relationship, any relationship, or who have a series of unhappy affairs, the prospect of some form of relationship is preferable to the isolation ward of 20th century loneliness.

So are happy, enduring relationships simply a matter of random luck and lucky breaks?

This would hardly be the basis for living a life that you love. So, how do you make your relationships work for you?

205

The fact is, deepening love takes practice, but we don't allow ourselves to make mistakes. That's often because we're terrified of losing the person we love, and also because we get ourselves into an "in-out" situation. We're either in love, or we're out of love; in a relationship, or out of a relationship.

No one would start to practise tennis, or try to improve their game, if they were not allowed to drop the ball. None of us would learn to swim if we hadn't spluttered in the water. Nobody learns to drive without stalling the engine and juddering to a halt.

It is the same with love, and the thoughts we have about our relationships. We need to be patient with ourselves. We need to be gentle with ourselves. We need to be able to laugh a little. And, above all, we need to be able to trust our yearning that we can be loved deeply and forever, and not make ourselves unavailable by becoming cynical, or deeply pessimistic.

Generally, there is one thing - and only one thing - that stops us from enjoying the best of loving relationships. And it is this: we won't forgive.

We just find it impossible to let go of the past - generally, our version of the past, and forgive someone. This doesn't make us wrong, or evil, or foolish. It is the way we are. But we are not hardwired to be like that; we can learn to be different.

Sometimes, we have to slay the dragon of loneliness. It prowls around our life breathing flames that burn up our self-confidence and self-worth. And unless we do something about it, we will be devoured by the dragon, and we will become even more isolated and lonely than we may feel.

But the dragon - like all bad dreams - is only a mirage that appears real. And, like a bad dream, we created it. When the dragon is banished, we realise how much it prevented anyone from entering our life. And the way to it is simply to let it go.

However don't leave an empty space or it will return. Little by little, you will need to begin to attract love back into your life. You do this by putting love where you feel there is none. In this way you will draw love into your life.

Too often, we frighten attractive people, and therefore love, away because we give the impression that we want to be alone! We've become so disenchanted by broken promises, hurt, or unhappiness, that we give out the wrong signals without realising. We may not go around with a long face ("she seems so happy" or "he is so successful") because we have learned to disguise and mask our real feelings of isolation.

Whenever two people meet there are really six present. There is each man as he sees himself, each as the other person sees him, and each man as he really is

William James

Learning to forgive and let go of hurtful thoughts isn't always easy. After all, sometimes it can seem that you are right to hate someone. Haven't they treated you badly? Wasn't their behaviour terrible? How could he? How dare she?

These bitter thoughts will continue to bubble and swirl in your mind until and unless you turn the heat down and let them go.

207

Letting go takes practice. Just by "thinking" once or twice a week will not work. And because hurtful thoughts bubble back again, you get discouraged and think it is a waste of time. Then you're back in the "learning to give up" loop. What you have to do is to begin to choose to let go of these negative thoughts, and keep on doing so, and not be surprised that you need to keep gently practising. Forgiveness is the superhighway to true, lasting love.

What you are doing, in fact, is un-learning what you may have thought for a year, or several years. So don't be surprised if it takes longer than you would like to regain a sense of balance and perspective. Be gentle with yourself, and turn the heat down!

There is something else you can learn to do in order to deepen your relationships and your love. You have to learn to trust. You have to let go of your negative self-fulfilling prophecies: "I'll never find anyone"; "men only want one thing"; "she would never like me"; "our marriage can't be saved".

You have to learn to trust that there may be an alternative, a possibility so unlikely (or so it seems) that you think you can't even think it!

Here are some "unthinkable" possibilities:

I am beautiful/attractive.

I really am sexy - just as I am.

Women/men like being around me.

My relationship is getting better and better.

I will find the perfect woman/man.

I can be incredibly happy and fulfilled on my own.

Perhaps there is another "unthinkable" possibility that is real for you.

Now, it takes practice to learn to trust. So often, because we live in an instantaneous age, we believe that just by thinking a thought, the action will occur. For example, you can think "I will find the perfect woman/man" once, and be surprised when 10 minutes later you are filled with gloom! In practice, you need to learn to approach the doubts and difficulties you encounter in your love and our relationships much more sensitively.

What you can do is to gently keep reminding yourself what the possibility of love means for you, and keep it in the front of your mind, and in your heart. You will find that it acts like a magnet. And all it takes is trust.

Trust is another key that unlocks the door to love. This happens in three stages.

If you could only love enough, you could be the most powerful person in the world

Emmett Fox

First, you need to trust your awareness, and trust your judgement, and trust in the reality of the situation where you feel there is no love. Don't judge yourself; don't judge someone else; don't judge the future or make a lifelong decision that nothing is going to work out. Instead, trust a little.

Now, this may seem impossible to do. But be gentle with yourself, the situation, and the other person - if someone else is involved.

What you are doing is trusting more in the reality of what is happening, and less in your interpretation.

Next, trust yourself to put love into the situation. In other words, rather than expect that you will somehow find love tied up in a parcel on a park bench for you to undo like a birthday present, you can begin putting love out.

It may be that you can put no more than a breadcrumb of love out but it is a beginning. Put love about in your life. Put love in your flat, in your bedroom, on your fridge door. Put love into your day by writing the word "love" on the back of cheques, or banknotes. Put love into a card you send to someone that you have been meaning to write to for ages but have not got around to doing so. If someone against whom you hold a grudge is unexpectedly pleasant, put love in return. Be civil, smile. Don't rush to judgement.

Finally, the result will be that you will draw love out from where it has been hiding. Because that it what love does in our life. It is like a shadow - it is always there, but sometimes it draws back. And often it is because we have frightened love away, without realising or wanting to.

All we need to do, where there is no love, is put love, and we will draw love out.

Question: When you say that forgiveness is the superhighway to love, do you mean that I just don't worry about the past? I mean, there are some people I've treated really badly. Do I just forget about it?

Answer: There's a world of difference between forgiving and forgetting. If you just forget about the people you say you hurt, then you are saying they don't matter, and you don't care - which isn't terribly loving, and won't draw love towards you. But forgiveness is different. Although you are letting go of the heaviness of the past, it doesn't mean that the pain you feel disappears. But it won't have the same meaning for you. There's a parallel with a broken limb that is stronger when it heals, although the scar may still be there. In the same way, if there is no way that you can make up with those people - and there may not be - you can really grow by letting go of the past, really forgiving them, and also forgiving yourself. And this may be something that you need to learn to do every day until it is real for you.

Question: I have had two abortions. I feel terrible about it, and often think about my babies. I find it impossible to forgive myself, or to let go of the past in the way you suggest. What can I do?

Answer: Sometimes there are events in our lives which are extremely hard for us to manage effectively on our own without guidance from someone we trust, and who cares deeply for us. It could be that you will really find help from a skilled professional who can help you lay to rest your burdens. It's what your children would want you to do for them. Right now, it seems impossible to forgive yourself, or to let go of the past. So don't try. What happened, happened. But gently, slowly, allow the past to be part of your present. In other words, maybe spend some meditation time with your thoughts about your hurt and sorrow and pain. Don't dwell unduly on them, but allow them in. Real growth, and maturity, occurs as we are able to look in the mirror and accept ourselves, warts and all, with all the upsets and mistakes that are reflected back at us. From what you have described, your heart is capable of great love. Much has been asked of you - much love is still awaiting you.

Question: I'm desperate! All I want is a partner, but the right person never seems to be around. I get so depressed about it. I just don't know if I'm ever going to find the right person.

Answer: It's very hard, isn't it? At times like this life does seem to be a complete fog without any reference point. In our developed society, not knowing is probably the most threatening and depressing experience. Because most of our waking activity consists in converting not knowing into knowing, we are wholly confronted when something happens - such as never seeming to find the right person as you've described - that we don't seem to know the answer to. It is possible, however, to navigate your way through the fog and pierce the cloud. It's done by learning to handle your emotions so that you never give up. Never, never give up on love. Don't settle for less: you are worth so much more than you can ever imagine. And that longing for love will attract the best of partners.

Summary

We can deepen our relationships by learning to forgive.

We often need to let go of negative, self-fulfilling prophecies.

When we put love out, we draw love into our lives.

Twentieth Morning

For Those in Their 60s and 70s

The ultimate decades of life can be the best of times, and they can be the worst of times.

Older people can enjoy the best of years because so many of the contradictions of life can be reconciled. What seems intolerable to a younger person can be viewed from a different perspective: a parent's anguish can be replaced with a grandparent's compassion. Rather than seeing goals not attained and a lifetime of roads not taken as failures or setbacks, the wider landscape of experience lends wisdom and serenity, and an enviable level of self-acceptance.

As we live longer, we have opportunities to develop interests that might have been impossible in the forging of a career or the raising of a family. It is not unusual for someone who feared that they would remain single to meet the partner of their dreams.

But, of course, the rose garden has thorns. Ill health can become a more frequent guest; the greying of hair and your changing appearance can appear to accelerate the sense of change; lapses of memory remind you that biological cellular rejuvenation can no longer be taken for granted.

Above all, in this final scene of the human drama, living a life that you love will depend on how you face the challenge of physical decline and your approach to death.

It would be a mistake to imagine - if you are not yet retired - that you can leave your responses to all of those challenges until then. Because how you will be in the future depends a great deal on how you are now!

If you don't look after your body now, why should you be surprised if it creaks and groans more than you want later? If you don't take an interest in life and living now, should you be surprised that your retirement becomes a (literal) mind-less round of golf, bridge and re-unions?

How do older people live lives that they love?

A key area is how we relate to health, illness, and the medical profession. Research shows that people who are compliant and quick to give in to authority recover less quickly from serious surgery than those who are feisty and demand an alternative opinion.

Try to be at peace with yourself, and help others share that peace. If you contribute to other people's happiness, you will find the true goal, the meaning of life

The Dalai Lama

So it could be that you need to learn to be more questioning, more sensitive to what your body is telling us, rather than trust blindly in health professionals.

Rather that rely exclusively on conventional medicines, why not find out more about complementary treatments for sleeplessness or tiredness, such as aromatherapy and reflexology?

Generally, health is often something that we have learned to give up on. Maybe there is a recurring complaint that you have decided is "just the way it is" and will not go away or get better. The chances are that it is, perhaps, 15 years since you actively investigated possible treatments.

Again, there can be personal ailments that you are embarrassed about: anything below the tummy button and above the thigh can often be a source of confusion and worry for years until they are sorted out.

It is known that men are far slower than women to seek professional advice when their health suffers, and particularly reluctant to take expert opinion as soon as they notice any physical change.

While women are, generally, more at ease with their bodies and find it easier to talk to their doctor, there can still be a fear of the worst which leads to delay, worry, anxiety, and possible worsening of what could have been dealt with easily at its early stages.

And, when it comes to serious, life-threatening illness - cancer, for instance - we can find ourselves paralysed with fear. We immediately jump to the worst outcome: it's malignant, I have six weeks to live, I'm going to DIE.

The reality - apart from the fact that we are all going to die - as every health professional will tell you, is that we tend only to hear of the bad news, and not of the many hundreds of people who recover and get better.

So, make certain that you have regular health checks, and enjoy learning to be feisty and difficult, rather than willing to please. It may be their timetable, but it's your life!

And, how about our own death ? How are we prepared to move on from this dazzling, glittering world of ours? Is it something that we think about, or shun? Are we at ease, grateful for the opportunities we have enjoyed, or terrified of dying?

Let's look at the fear we have. First - it's natural. Fear of death seems to be a biological reaction that preserves our species. But there is more than that. We can be afraid of pain, of losing our faculties. Maybe we have terrifying thoughts of being certified dead when we aren't.

All this is Level Two behaviour, where we lack the information that we need.

Find a professional who specialises in this information. Discover what you need to know about the management of pain if this is a worry for you.

Maybe there is another level to your thinking: that your spiritual gauge is low. But there are so many opportunities to reflect and think about God, heaven, Buddha, Allah.

Grow old with me.
The best is yet to be

Robert Browning

Have you made a will? Do you want to? Do you have strong feelings about your funeral? Is there a special reading or hymn that you would like?

Is there unfinished business that you want to complete? Something that needs to be said that, until now, has been unsaid? You don't have to, but sometimes it is the older person who can make the first move, and by doing so, open up a torrent of love where affection has been frozen.

And, you can now enjoy the love and affection of many, many people.

Twenty-first evening

Living Your Future Now

When we come back from holiday, turn the key in the lock and open the door we might feel regret that our vacation is over, relief at coming home, exhaustion from the flight, but we're back! No matter how exciting our holiday, life goes on. And after a holiday we're different. We have had great weather; we relaxed; the resort/guide/facilities were superb. We come home determined not to lost that "feel great, must keep" feeling.

But, we do lose it. The tan fades, and after the first hour of the first day back at work it can seem that we have never been away at all.

Choosing to live the life you love is like that. You glimpse the possibility that you can live a truly fabulous life; there are moments as you reflect on what you have learned, and how you can continue learning, when, suddenly, what seemed out of the question, beyond reality even, can NEVER happen, becomes possible.

And then the "old" same-as-it-was chilly breeze blows in your face, and you shut up the windows on the life you love.

You have been here before. But by now, you are not surprised; nor do you get angry or depressed with yourself, because you recognise and smile at your professionalism at "giving up".

You now know what is needed to move from Level Two to Levels Three and Four. You just need to remember that we are all beginners, and that we do not have to be perfect. Practice does not have to make you perfect, but it will shift you quickly on the road to deep and lasting happiness.

But you need more. You need something more than a book, or a computer programme. You need something inside yourself that you can always draw upon for support and strength when you are faced with setbacks or surprises that throw you - momentarily - off balance.

Earlier in this journey we looked at "scaffolding" that can support us: sacred spaces and loving mementoes.

On this last day together we will travel inwardly, and develop even more powerful and effective strategies for supporting you in your personal growth and strength.

We will discover the power of Inner Beliefs.

When you believe something, you accept that it is "true". And when life is "true" for us, everything fits together in alignment. One profound consequence of living the life that we love is that your beliefs are utterly in alignment with what you experience.

Create your future from your future,
not your past

Werner Erhard

There are no upsets; no heartache; no enduring grief; no "poor me".

Over the last 21 days you have begin to change the habits you have learned over your lifetime. You have learned to be gentle with yourself, to relax, to take yourself a little less seriously, and to begin to play with the outrageous idea that when someone knocks on your door, there is no-one at home!

A belief then, is a way of thinking that works to make sense of the world. And all beliefs are provisional and temporary. The mistake is to think that your beliefs are forever. As you change, you need to develop your thinking as you grow and mature.

Never confuse your beliefs with "what" you believe in. So many people lose their sense of what is sacred in their lives because their way of thinking about the world (the "religious" belief) got left behind. Just as you outgrow clothes you wore as children, you outgrow ways of understanding the world that were appropriate when you were younger, but which are of less or no value, as adults: Santa Claus, the tooth fairy, or God with a white beard.

A belief in X is a shorthand expression for, "At the moment, this is the most useful way to think about X." AND TO GO ON THINKING ABOUT X - not to give up and say, OK - that's it.

There are three, powerful Inner Beliefs that relate to living the life you love.

A belief in acting with integrity

A belief in loving tenderly

A belief in personal transformation

Let's look at how you can develop and deepen each of these beliefs.

A belief in acting with integrity

There is a Zen proverb: "When you walk, walk. When you sit, sit. Whatever you do, don't wobble." Integrity is like that. When you speak with integrity, you won't lie, you won't prevaricate, you won't say one thing and mean another. If you say "X" the person listening to you will know deep down that "X" will happen.

Integrity isn't something that you're born with, or not. Integrity is something that you have to learn, and decide to use every day of your life. Abraham Lincoln said, "Whatever you are, be a good one." Whatever you do, wherever you are, your integrity will attract the best in others, and will bring out the best in you. Integrity works to allow you to lead a life that makes a difference, and that is a gift to others.

A belief in loving tenderly

In the end, this is probably the only thing that matters. There are miles of bookshelves about love, but probably every one of us

There is no end. There is no beginning.
There is only the infinite passion of life

Frederico Fellini

knows from day to day when we love, and when we don't. Does it happen naturally? Not really. You have to renew each day in love, and keep on doing it. Does it get easier? Maybe. But you can choose every day to make your life a place where love goes to work. At any one moment, your physical heart is contracting and expanding, pumping life-giving blood around your body. In the same way, your "loving heart" is either contracting, or expanding. You're either orientating yourself towards other people, or you are contracting inwardly.

When you love tenderly, you go gently on ourselves, not putting yourself down when you don't meet the standards and values that matter to you, but sticking with it.

When you love tenderly, you learn to understand other people's situation when they let you down: when they say hurtful words, when they no longer seem to share the values that matter to you.

When you love tenderly, you learn to let go of cherished opinions so as to open yourself to other possibilities that may, at first, seem alien to you.

When you love tenderly, you don't cling to certainties and fixed positions. You allow a measure of humility to influence your self perception. Maybe - just maybe - you're not right all the time!

A belief in personal transformation

Gandhi said that individuals needed to become the change they wanted to see in the world. So often, we expect others to change, and are slower to accept that probably our need to change is greater!

We all know that at a physical level our bodies are continually changing: cells divide and multiply, tissue breaks down and renews, and every seven years our entire body is different to that which was before. The challenge is for our mental and spiritual faculties to keep up!

We need to nurture our belief in personal transformation with supportive practices. Read books that develop your self-awareness; listen to tapes; take part in seminars that offer genuine insight; bookmark Internet sites that are helpful.

Do not expect everyone to share your views; people move in different directions and grow in different ways at different rates and at different times. Become extremely tolerant and forgiving of others, and remain true to your own values and standards.

Ralph Waldo Emerson wrote these words:

> *To laugh often and much;*
> *to win the respect of intelligent people*
> *and the affection of children;*
> *to earn the appreciation of honest critics*
> *and endure the betrayal of false friends;*
> *to appreciate beauty, to find the best in others;*
> *to leave the world a little bit better,*
> *whether by a healthy child,*
> *a garden path or a redeemed social condition;*
> *to know even one life has breathed easier*
> *because you have lived.*

It wouldn't be a bad legacy, would it?

The fact is, you can live your future now. At any one moment you can choose to fully live your life now, not live a half-life dominated by the past, or live a half-life waiting in life's bus station for a coach that's been cancelled!

You really do have the vision, resources, talent and wisdom to live the life you love.

Why wait any longer?

Books you can use

Books you can use

The Aladdin Factor - Jack Canfield and Mark Victor Hansen

Awaken the Giant Within - Anthony Robbins

Feel the Fear and Do It Anyway - Susan Jeffers

Men are From Mars, Women are From Venus - John Gray

The Seven Laws of Spiritual Success - Deepak Chopra

Anatomy of the Spirit - Caroline Myss

Born to Win - Muriel James and Dorothy Jongward

The Artist's Way - Julia Cameron

8 Weeks to Optimum Health - Andrew Weil

The Art of Happiness - HH the Dalai Lama

You Can Heal Your Life - Louise Hay

The Little Book of Calm - Paul Wilson

The Tibetan Book of Living and Dying - Sogyal Pinpoche

What Colour is Your Parachute? - Bolles

The Road Less Travelled - Scott Peck

Superfoods - Straten and Griggs

Pulling Your Own Strings - Wayne Dyer

Creative Visualisation - Gawain

The Relaxation and Stress Reduction Workbook - Davis/Eshelman

Exercise

Try out something new: find out about

Yoga, Dance, Cycling, Jogging, Aerobics, Swimming, Tai-Chi, Sports.

Groups

Attend an introductory session offered by The Landmark Corporation, Insight, Avatar, Mastery, all 12 Step Programs.

Psychological development

Discover more about NLP, TA, Dream work, keeping a Journal, Jung, Astrology, the Tarot, Hypnosis.

Websites You Can Visit

www.jamesgladwin.com (to be registered)

Steven Covey ("7 Habits"):
http://www.franklincovey.com/

Anthony Robbins ("Awaken the Giant Within"):
http://www.tonyrobbins.com/

Richard Bandler (Co-Founder of NLP):
http://www.nlp-dhe.com/

Dan Millman ("Way of the Peaceful Warrior"):
http://www.danmillman.com/

Richard Bach ("Jonathan Livingstone Seagull"):
http://www.richardbach.com/

Louise L. Hay ("You can heal your life"):
http://www.louisehayteachers.com/

Susan Jeffers ("Feel the fear and do it anyway"):
http://www.susanjeffers.com/